MAKING SEARCH WORK

MAKING SEARCH WORK

Implementing Web, Intranet and Enterprise Search

Martin White

Information Today, Inc.
Medford, New Jersey

Making Search Work:
Implementing Web, Intranet and Enterprise Search

First published in the U.K. by Facet Publishing, 2007. This simultaneous U.S. publication 2007.

 This edition published by Information Today, Inc., 143 Old Marlton Pike, Medford, New Jersey 08055.

Library of Congress Cataloging-in-Publication Data

White, Martin S. (Martin Scott), 1948-
Making search work : implementing Web, intranet and enterprise search / Martin White.
p. cm.
Includes bibliographical references and index.
ISBN 978-1-57387-305-5
1. Search engines. 2. Intranets (Computer networks) 3. Knowledge management. 4. Business enterprises—Computer networks. I. Title.
ZA4230W48 2007
025.04—dc22

2007003335

Printed and bound in Great Britain.

To

Cynthia, Nick and Simon

Contents

Foreword

Why do you need a book about search? Isn't search easy? A searcher enters some text into a box, clicks a button, and hey presto! - all the pertinent information appears in a nice handy list. Google made it simple; why can't your company do the same?

It turns out that effective search is complicated - and hard. Ask any enterprise knowledge manager, website owner, e-commerce director, or, really, any fellow employee, 'Are you satisfied with your search engine?' The responses will catalogue a litany of woes: 'It gives the wrong answers'; 'We don't understand how it works'; 'It doesn't find all of our information'; 'It's slow'; 'The results are cluttered and irrelevant.'

This is often followed by the almost inevitable kicker: 'We're investigating new search technology to fix it.'

Yet technology is rarely the problem. Although people have been searching electronic information for more than four decades, search as a discipline remains quite young. You have significant choices about what technologies to apply and how to deploy them. Security, usability, scalability, and information architecture all present complicated, but important, challenges. Enterprises that succeed at search address these challenges as an ongoing process rather than a discrete technology project.

That's why you need this book.

I can think of no one better than Martin White to create a business-person's guide to good search practices. As a search expert of global repute (and outlook!), Martin has taken the time and care to condense a complicated topic into an easy read. There are a variety of different technical approaches to search in the marketplace, but this book is essential to any search manager.

Tony Byrne
CMSWatch.com

Preface

Over the last few years search has come centre-screen, thanks largely to Google, a company less than ten years old but with a market capitalization that is already 30% of that of Microsoft. Entering just one or two words into the search box is the entry point to relevant websites containing billions of pages of information. It all seems so easy. Look behind the scenes and you begin to realize the scale of the operation and the degree of innovation. The applied mathematics of Google takes a book to begin to comprehend, and then there are probably a million or more servers located in secure bunkers. There is a similar story behind Yahoo! and Microsoft, and the other public web search services. The result is that the public web search services do a remarkably good job in sifting through millions of websites to highlight those that could be of some relevance.

By comparison, searching for information in the digital repositories inside organizations is usually very difficult, with employees having lost faith in their intranet because of ineffective search, and visitors to the organization's website are hindered rather than helped by the search functionality. A search for the term 'intranet' on a UK central government website returned files with titles that included File30958, Microsoft Word - errs32.doc, file 22013, Business Case and Sarah in the top ten relevant documents.

It is an often-quoted suggestion that 80% of the information created by an organization is unstructured. Whatever the real answer is, there is now a general concern that the rate of growth is so great that the problems of finding specific information are now among the most serious challenges faced by an organization of any size. Many organizations have adopted content management software to manage the addition of content into websites and intranets, but have found that the distributed authorship that this software encourages makes information discovery even more difficult. Information on search volumes in organizations is not easy to come by, but certainly in one major pharmaceutical company over 4500 searches a day are carried out on its global intranet. No matter how good the site navigation is for a website or intranet, there is always benefit to the user and the organization from effective search functionality. When search works well it seems almost like magic. When it works badly then the discontent of a site visitor or an employee up against a deadline can put the objectives of the organization at risk.

This book is the first to address the issue of ensuring that search works for an organization, be it on PC desktops, the corporate website, one or many intranets, and then at an enterprise search level. Achieving this is not easy. To a greater extent than is the case with content management software, search has to be a joint project between IT and the business units, as the hardware and network requirements of search software can be quite demanding. The design of the user interface has to be intuitive for a range of different users, and even once installed search software needs to be 'tuned' to ensure that the most relevant information is found, no matter how much or how little searchers may know about the subject of their search.

This book is divided into two main sections. In the first there is an outline of how search software works, advice on specifying and selecting search software, ensuring that the full performance of the software is obtained, and that the user interfaces are intuitive. The section includes brief profiles of search software companies. The second section deals with some of the specific issues of implementing desktop, website, intranet and enterprise search software, including a ten-step project plan for website and intranet search. The challenges of searching in multiple languages are also considered.

Although search is high technology and makes use of sophisticated mathematics, this book assumes no technical knowledge. My objective is to provide information and advice to anyone tasked with implementing or improving their organization's search applications. The origins of search technology date back to the early 1960s, but the industry is still in its infancy compared to many other sectors of the IT software business. This is going to change significantly over the next few years as organizations realize the risks they are running in not having effective search solutions: work duplicated, time wasted, market opportunities missed, compliance audits failed, and visitors going to other sites to buy products and services.

Search has to work.

Does yours?

Martin White

Acknowledgements

An invitation from Nancy Garman (Information Today Inc.) to present the Keynote Address at the inaugural Enterprise Search Summit in New York in 2004 made me realize how little published information there was on enterprise search. A return invitation to present at the 2006 Enterprise Search Summit was very useful in clarifying the scope of this book.

Another important catalyst for this book came from an invitation from Jakob Nielsen (Nielsen Norman Group) to present a workshop on intranet search at the company's User Experience 2005 events in Boston and London in October/November 2005. In devising the 2006 version of this workshop the title *Making Search Work* emerged as a way of setting out the scope of the workshop, and now this book. In 2005 William Hann (Freepint) generously published *The Enterprise Search Guidebook* which unknowingly served as a pilot version of this book.

Howard McQueen (McQueen Consulting), Jed Cawthorne (The Open University) and Jane McConnell (NetStrategyJMC) made invaluable comments on an initial draft of this book. James Robertson (Step Two Designs) has been immensely supportive of the concept of this book and undertook an invaluable line-by-line review of the text. I have learned a great deal from Steven Arnold (ArnoldIT), the doyen of search gurus. Karen Blakeman gave me a great deal of assistance on desktop search.

I am grateful to Margaret O'Donnell (Royal National Institute of the Blind) and Jessica Rutt (Nature Publishing Group) for readily giving permission to reproduce the screen shots in Chapter 7.

Notes

Any reference to a search engine vendor in this report is solely for the purpose of illustration, and does not imply a recommendation by Intranet Focus Ltd.

Research for this book, including the verification of web citations, was completed in December 2006.

Making search work – critical success factors

Critical success factor	Read about it in	
Search has to be placed in context with other routes to information discovery.	Chapter 1	Search must work
From the outset a broad-based project team and a senior-level sponsor are essential, because of the range of knowledge and skills required to develop the initial specification and then to evaluate the products.	Chapter 4 Chapter 5	Making a business case for search Specifying and selecting a search engine
Understand how the various search engine applications work, so that not only is the best choice made at the outset but future requirements can also be met.	Chapter 2 Chapter 3 Chapter 6 Chapter 13	How search works The search business Optimizing search performance Future directions
Organizations need to assess their requirements for web, desktop, intranet and enterprise search on a strategic basis, linked to business requirements.	Chapter 1 Chapter 8 Chapter 9 Chapter 10 Chapter 11	Search must work Desktop search Implementing web search Implementing search for an intranet Enterprise search
In any organization there will be a range of different search requirements from users. These need to be identified through the development of personas and search scenarios.	Chapter 5	Specifying and selecting a search engine
All search software products index documents, run queries against the index, and then present the results of the search to the user. Understanding how this is carried out is important.	Chapter 2 Chapter 7	How search works Search usability
Most enterprise installations start small and then grow. The implications of scaling up the indexing process and extending the functionality (for example for multiple languages) need to be assessed at the outset, and kept under close review.	Chapter 11 Chapter 12	Enterprise search Multilingual search
Providing a high degree of usability for the search interface is essential.	Chapter 7	Search usability
A search engine needs to be continually monitored to ensure that search performance targets are achieved and changing user requirements are met.	Chapter 6	Optimizing search performance

Chapter 1

Search must work

In this chapter:

- The evidence that search can have a significant impact on business performance
- A brief history of the development of search technology
- Understanding how people go about searching
- The potential for the role of information discovery manager

Searching but not finding

In July 2005 the Quarterly Survey from McKinsey Consulting[1] reported on the Global Executive Survey that the company had conducted among 7800 executives in 132 countries, a fifth of them at Chief Executive Officer (CEO) or Chief Information Officer (CIO) level. Overall, 29% of CEO/CIO-level respondents and 40% of other senior managers reported that it was difficult to find information on which to make company-wide decisions. This is a very worrying finding. Companies are flying blind, and making highly risky decisions without being able to find information that they have already created and stored.

Among many others was a survey carried out in 2004 by Vascom Bourne on behalf of Inxight Software among IT Directors in the UK financial services sector. According to the survey:

- 73% of respondents said that the main barrier knowledge workers face in sharing corporate information was not being able to use one information retrieval tool to capture data across several repositories.
- 58% of respondents also said that their company's search tools were ineffective at sourcing information quickly and efficiently.
- 66% of the companies interviewed said employees were regenerating information simply because they were unaware that the documents already existed.

For a number of years Susan Feldman and her colleagues in the Content Management and Retrieval Solutions research group of IDC (International Data Corporation)[2] have been surveying the time taken to undertake a range of office tasks. Their latest analysis indicates that, on average, an office worker spends 9.5 hours a week searching for information, but, of this time, 3.5 hours is wasted in not being able to find the information required. As a result, either this information has to be recreated or a decision must be made on the basis of inadequate information.

A major change over the last decade or so is that the value of unstructured, text-based information has increased substantially as organizations strive to enhance their competitive position through information and knowledge. The days when an organization depended solely on information contained in highly structured databases of client information are long gone.

The situation is getting worse by the day, a result of a continuing increase in the use of e-mail to circulate documents, the growth of content being published on an intranet through the adoption of content management software, and the need to ensure that an organization is compliant with governance regulations, such as Freedom of Information legislation and the Sarbanes-Oxley requirements. In the post-Enron business world not being able to produce documents showing that an organization has acted within relevant governance standards and guidelines could have very serious implications for that organization. The risks arising from not being able to find information are very great indeed.

E-mails are a major source of information loss. Even if the information contained in an attached document is available from a file server, the e-mail itself usually contains a wealth of knowledge about the contents of the document, perhaps reminding readers that the table on page 6 has the wrong units on one of the axes, or highlighting a website that would provide background information on the subjects covered by the document.

All this is lost if e-mails cannot be searched. Many companies are reluctant to do this because employees also use e-mail for personal purposes, and perhaps for criticizing others in the organization. Because of the lack of a clear and enforced policy on e-mail use, the organization is at serious risk from not being able to find the information and knowledge contained in e-mail messages.

Even where there is currently some search function on a website or an intranet the organization acknowledges that it does not work and yet fails to do anything about the situation. The problem is that Google has brought search centre-screen, and provides a search benchmark that few can match or even aspire to. But users of websites and of intranets now expect there to be good search functionality, and when this is lacking begin to wonder just how committed the organization is to meeting visitor and employee expectations.

The level of investment by organizations in search technology is still very low. The current world market for information retrieval software is only around $700 million, which in IT market terms is very small indeed. Sales of enterprise resource planning software applications are running at an annual level of $20 billion.

What are the reasons for this state of affairs? Some clues can be found in a survey carried out in late 2005 by the Ark Group of over 500 companies.[3] The chief obstacles to developing an effective search and retrieval strategy were cited as (in decreasing order of priority):

- lack of metadata and poor metadata management
- taxonomy development and maintenance
- integration with existing systems

- legacy databases and applications
- demonstrating return on investment
- teaching staff effective search techniques
- securing senior management buy-in
- geographically distributed infrastructure and content.

The issue that becomes apparent from this list is that the solutions to these problems do not lie within the ambit of any one department or Board member, so finding a search champion is very difficult. Certainly IT departments have an important role to play, but are not likely to have the detailed knowledge of the business requirements to select the optimum solution, and of course have probably never selected search software before.

Senior managers are likely to say that all they want is Google, which of course they can now have, even if the search algorithms are different from those used in the Google web search engine. Among business units the requirements of human resources (HR), sales, marketing, planning, research, customer services, and indeed any other department are not only likely to be different but to be expressed in different ways, and in the end it becomes clear that there is very little understanding of why and how people search for information.

One of the key issues with search is that people should trust it. One project we undertook for a major financial institution gained a 55% response rate from employees, and this was probably because we asked them if they trusted the search feature on the organization's intranet. The clear answer was No! If search is not trusted then it will not be used. There is no point in someone searching for information and finding that the search implementation is not giving results they can trust. In a website the visitor will move to another site, and inside an organization either the work will be redone or time will be wasted e-mailing or phoning around for the information.

The objective of this book is to ensure that benefits, risks and issues around desktop, website and enterprise search are fully appreciated.

The use of computers to search through text documents is not new, and indeed the origins of the way in which most of the current search products work can be traced back to technology innovations on online bibliographic search services in the 1960s and 1970s. Many of the lessons learned by these search pioneers seem not to have been taken into account.

The advent of Eureka

In 1980 Sir Tim Berners-Lee had the moment of inspiration that led to his initial development of hypertext, but it was a decade later that he realized how the internet could be used to create a worldwide web of information. The first website[4] was set up at CERN and went online on 6 August 1991. It provided information about what the world wide web was, and described the basic features of a browser and a web server. The simplicity of the concept soon led to a rapid growth of websites, and a concomitant growth in indexes to these sites to enable users to find information. However, website growth soon expanded so rapidly that the indexes could not keep up with the situation.

Boston, Massachusetts, could arguably lay claim to being the epicentre of the information revolution. Much of the early development of the internet took place in the Boston area in the early 1960s, and in 1994 Berners-Lee founded the the World Wide Web Consortium (W3C) at the Massachusetts Institute of Technology. At the same time Digital Equipment Corporation (DEC), based not many miles away from MIT, were wondering just what to do with a very high-performance chip set they had developed and codenamed Alpha.[5] Although the performance was quite outstanding, so was the amount of heat that the chip gave off, and that was a major problem for commercial deployment. The solution came from Paul Flaherty, a research engineer working for DEC in Palo Alto, who realized that the power of the Alpha chip could be harnessed in servers that would search the web. In December 1995 DEC launched their AltaVista search engine. This used a fast, multithreaded crawler and an efficient search back-end running on the Alpha-based servers. At the time of launch it had crawled and indexed 16 million pages. Yahoo! had been launched a few months earlier, but at that time was primarily using well established concepts of categorization to provide access to the web.

Of course, using computers to search for information was nothing new. As is now recognized, much of the fundamental work was carried out in the UK during World War 2 by the code-breaking community at Bletchley Park, and by the early 1960s the first online information retrieval systems were in the prototype stage. However, these systems were designed to be used by information professionals steeped in Boolean algebra and with the training to be able to evaluate the information that the systems presented them with. Much of the innovation that led to these services came out of System Development Corporation, in particular from Carlos Cuadra, and also from Lockheed, where Roger Summit played a key role. Both companies launched commercial services in 1972.[6] These search services also came at a cost, because apart from connection and processing costs the publishers who owned the databases were entitled to a royalty.

With the advent of the web, where information was published free, a different approach was not only possible but essential. AltaVista changed the model and put search at the disposal of anyone with a connection to the web, who could search as many times as they wished to without charge.

For various reasons AltaVista gradually lost its market dominance, a process that was accelerated by the launch in 1998 of Google, with its innovative approach to the ranking of relevant search results. Google brought search centre-screen, and through some very sophisticated server technology and some very neat applied mathematics created a totally scalable service that now indexes billions of pages. For three decades from 1960 the top search experts worked in the IT industry with companies such as IBM and DEC. From the 1990s onward they have been working for Google, Yahoo! and Microsoft, a trio often known as GYM, and these are the companies that are setting the road-map for search technology and performance.

Of course, the work that was being undertaken at IBM and other IT companies was aimed at providing organizations with the ability to find information from the rapidly increasing collections of text documents being generated initially by word-processors and then PCs. The problems here are not on the scale of the web, but are equally challenging.

The four dimensions of search

There is a much-used matrix about knowledge that was famously used by former US Secretary of Defense Donald Rumsfeld in commenting on intelligence failures in the Iraq conflict. Search supports four knowledge functions:

- **We know what we know**. We use search even when we know the answer to a question. That is because we like to have the assurance that we have not been overtaken by events, and we can go into a meeting confident that we have found all the information arising from a particular project or business initiative.
- **We know what we don't know**. The core function of search has always been to help us add to the knowledge that we have. We don't know the date of the launch of Alta Vista, and we need to find out for a presentation that we are giving. The challenge here is to be able to tell the search engine what we do know, so that we don't end up with a lot of irrelevant information.
- **We don't know what we know**. Our memory is far from perfect, but often we need a pointer of some sort to jog our grey cells into action: 'Of course I know that - how could I forget?'
- **We don't know what we don't know**. The biggest challenge of all for a search engine is to help in situations where we don't know what we don't know. Amazon trades on this in a very clever way by suggesting books that other readers of the book of our choice have read, as a way of informing us about things we did not know. Clustering and visualization technologies can help alert us to areas of knowledge that we did not know existed.

In probably most circumstances search cannot be accomplished by a single query: the user has to have a dialogue with the search application that can sometimes turn out to be quite a random walk towards the eventual location of the information required. Marcia Bates has described this well in her berry-picking analogy, in which the searcher obtains an initial set of documents/information, considers them, and then constructs a new search statement.[7] Another, complementary, approach comes from Donna Maurer,[8] in which she proposes that there are four approaches to searching, which are set out in her seminal paper:

1 **Known-item**. Known-item information seeking is the easiest to understand. In a known-item task, the users:
   - know what they want
   - know what words to use to describe it
   - may have a fairly good understanding of where to start.
2 **Exploratory**. In an exploratory task, people have some idea of what they need to know. However, they may or may not know how to articulate it, and, if they can, they may not yet know the right words to use. They may not know where to start to look. They will usually recognize when they have found the right answer, but may not know whether they have found enough information.

   In this mode, the information need will almost certainly change as they discover information and learn, and the gap between their current knowledge and their target knowledge narrows.
3 **Don't know what you need to know**. The key concept behind this mode is that people often don't know exactly what they need to know. They may think they need one thing but they actually need another; or they may be looking at a website without a specific goal in mind.
4 **Re-finding**. This mode is relatively straightforward: people looking for things they have already seen. They may remember exactly where it is, remember what site it was on, or have little idea about where it was.

The alignment of this approach with the matrix above is very close. Another important study on the way in which people search for information has been the work on information scent by Chi and his colleagues at the Xerox Palo Alto Research Center (PARC)[9, 10]

In summary, designing effective search systems involves an excellent understanding of the way in which our brains process information, and in particular the limitations of short term memory. This issue of short term memory has a major impact on the design of search results pages.

Search is quite a complicated technology and, as is described in more detail in Chapter 2, comprises at a minimum:

- indexing
- query management
- ranking of results
- results formatting.

Every search vendor has their own views on the most effective way to undertake these four operations, which are all interlinked. Only through careful testing against sample sets of documents and queries, and then by constant tuning of the search engine, can the full effectiveness of the search engine be obtained. There is a need to support a dialogue with the search user, and usability has to come at the very top of the implementation process. The failure of many search implementations is that they assume that all users search the same way. The truth is that every user is different, as we are always looking to add to what we already know, and only we know what we know, provided we can remember what we know.

Findability

Over the last four decades a considerable amount of research has been carried out into all aspects of information retrieval, as even a cursory glance at journals such as the *Journal of Information Science* or a look through the papers at the annual Text Retrieval Conferences (TREC) will show.[11] There is a danger of taking search out of context. All too often the justification for implementing a search solution for a corporate website or an intranet is that people cannot find the information they want through the site navigation. Once search has been implemented, the alarming discovery is then made that there are some basic underlying issues of poor content management and metadata management, and all that the search engine has done is bring a magnifying glass to these issues.

Search must be part of a total information discovery strategy, and someone who has thought a lot about this issue is Peter Morville,[12] with his concept of 'findability'. This he defines as:

- the quality of being locatable or navigable
- the degree to which a particular object is easy to discover or locate

- the degree to which a system or environment supports navigation and retrieval.

In the end the requirement is to be able to find an object, be it a document, a piece of data or a video file. There are only three information discovery routes:

- lists, indexes and classifications
- hyperlinking to related information
- searching through a computer-created index of all relevant metadata.

The challenge for any organization is to achieve the correct balance of these routes. A website represents a known collection of objects, and so much can be done through lists and indexes, and of course through hyperlinking. Search can be important, and is used either at the outset to reach the relevant area of a site quickly, or as a fallback when all else has failed.

When it comes to internal websites - intranets - hyperlinking is much less effective because of the heterogeneous nature of the content, a higher proportion of longer documents in formats other than HTML, and a distributed content authoring environment in which no single person has a sufficiently comprehensive knowledge of the collection to be able to decide where hyperlinks should be added. In intranets search is not a nice-to-have but a need-to-have.

Search and navigation

Search is not a solution to poor information architecture. Effective search has to be integrated within the overall information architecture of a website or an intranet, so that there is a seamless path between the structured navigation, hyperlinks and the search function. In presenting the results of a search it can be of value to include the URL of the displayed item in a way that enables the searcher to realize that there is a section of the site that they have not visited. This requires the URLs to be short, structured and intuitive, features that are often missing with the increased use of dynamic page publishing and portal applications where the URL also contains session information that is of no assistance with site discovery.

The implementation of a new search engine may require a redesign of the site, or at least sections of it, and this can add to the cost and implementation schedule of the release of the search function. However, just adding a new search box is not going to obtain the best return on the investment.

The role of the Information Discovery Manager

The information profession seems to be constantly trying to define a role for itself in 21st century organizations. Certainly many intranets are managed by information professionals, and they are also involved in websites. To do this they need new skills in websites technology, but they are missing an obvious opportunity, that is, to support the development of search within the organization - not just for the intranet, but across all applications and requirements. They already know how search should work, and they have the experience gained in working with online database services. They are heavily involved in web research, and understand how taxonomies and classifications can be used to enhance the information discovery process.

Indeed, the opportunity is there for a new position inside an organization, that of Information Discovery Manager. The scope is enormous and business-critical. The roles that are well suited to an information professional acting as Information Discovery Manager include:

- developing and maintaining taxonomies
- developing and supervising usability tests
- developing metadata schemas
- ensuring that external information resources are integrated into the search experience
- identifying 'best bets' documents for important searches
- identifying the scope of test collections of documents for use in the evaluation of search products
- managing the search 'helpdesk'

- monitoring developments in search technology and the search business
- reviewing search logs to develop search enhancements
- teaching staff effective search techniques.

The remainder are clearly the responsibility of the IT department, and with search in particular there is an important role for IT to provide an adequate technology infrastructure to support search applications.

References

1. www.mckinseyquarterly.com/home.aspx.
2. www.idc.com.
3. Ark Group (2005) *The Age of Search: intelligent retrieval and analysis*, London, Ark Group, www.ark-group.com.
4. http://info.cern.ch/.
5. www.washingtontechnology.com/news/10_23/news/10125-1.html.
6. Bourne, C. P. and Hahn, T. B. (2002) *A History of Online Information Services*, Cambridge MA, MIT Press.
7. www.gseis.ucla.edu/faculty/bates/berrypicking.html.
8. www.boxesandarrows.com/view/four_modes_of_seeking_information_and_how_to_design_for_them.
9. www2.parc.com/istl/groups/uir/publications/items/UIR-2001-07-Chi-CHI2001_InfoScentModel.pdf.
10. www.steptwo.com.au/papers/kmc_informationscent.index.html.
11. http://trec.nist.gov/.
12. Morville, P. (2005) *Ambient Findability*, Sebastopol CA, O'Reilly Publishing, www.oreilly.com.

Chapter 2

How search works

In this chapter:

- An explanation of how search software works
- The differences between ranking, relevance, precision and recall
- The value of a taxonomy
- How to ensure that document confidentiality is not compromised by a search engine

Introduction

In order to evaluate and implement a search application it is important to understand the basic elements of search technology, which form the basis of both search software and search application products. There are a number of distinct elements in the process, from capturing content to presenting it within a browser on demand:

- content definition
- indexing
- query management
- ranking of results

- results formatting
- document access.

The challenge in selecting a search application is that every vendor carries out these processes in a slightly different way. Understanding the similarities and differences between the products on the market is important in ensuring that user requirements are fully accommodated. A good understanding of search technology is also important when it comes to implementing and 'tuning' a search engine. There will be a continuing need to look at the types of search being carried out, and the results they obtain, and then changing various elements of the search process (especially the way in which ranking is carried out) to ensure that users obtain the maximum number of relevant results.

Content definition

The initial task is to define the content that needs to be searched, and hence indexed. For smaller applications the index is generated on the server that also contains the content to be indexed, a common situation with website searching. The search query is then run against this index. However, the index to a set of documents may typically be between 15 and 50% of the file size of the content collection and querying the index also requires a substantial amount of processing.

As a result the indexes and query management are accomplished on a separate server. A number of options are then available.

Option 1: manually move content onto the indexing server. This may well be appropriate when a document is being developed on a highly collaborative basis and there are multiple interim versions. Only when the final approved version is available might it then be moved onto the indexing server. This of course raises the issue of whether interim versions of a document should be indexed. Apart from procedural issues, it is important that the file naming and document metadata indicate that the document is indeed an interim version.

Option 2: use a spider to identify new content; this is the approach adopted by all public web search applications. Depending on the volume of new content and the capacity of the indexing process (a function of machine power and indexing technology), the spider might be programmed to visit each server on an hourly, daily, or some other specified basis. If a document is posted to the server just after the spider has checked for new ones it will be invisible to a search user until the next pass of the spider. Search engines usually contain a number of ways to enable the administrative team to ensure that content is crawled on an appropriate basis.

Option 3: install a script on each server that recognizes new content as it is added, and copies the document to the indexing server; this approach is used with Microsoft SharePoint 2007, where the process of saving a document means that it is automatically indexed.

A new challenge is presented by wikis, where content may be added in bursts around a particular discussion or virtual meeting. Here the pages may need to be indexed on an hourly basis, or perhaps even more frequently.

In most organizations there may be a need to use all three approaches for different types of content, and this can only be decided when there is a very thorough understanding of the rate at which documents containing specific types of content are added to the servers to match the expectations of users.

Indexing

At a basic level the process of indexing creates a file of every word in a way which ensures that a query can then be matched against any combination of these index terms, and documents containing the terms can thus be located. The indexing process has several elements. The first is to enable every word to be added to the list of keywords, and to be tagged with positional information about the relationship of that word to other words in the same sentence and the frequency of the word in the document itself. The location of the word in the document may also be identified by metadata tagging, so that a search can be restricted to words that appear in just the title or the summary of a document. The end result is what is described as an inverted index, and has long been the underlying database structure used for information retrieval. The underlying mathematics involves the use of hash tables to enable indexes to be rebuilt with the minimum of time and processing power when new information has to be indexed. The optimization of these tables is one of the fundamental innovations in Google's PageRank approach.[1]

The amount of positional information associated with each word is a major factor in the size of the index files that are created. The size of the index varies with the type of content, but in general will probably be between 15% and 50% of the total volume of content indexed.

However, just indexing the words that appear in the document is only part of the process to provide an effective search. There may be a requirement to match the keywords against a corporate taxonomy so as to provide a range of synonyms, and to be able to interpret concepts that do not appear in the document itself, such as 'governance' or 'product development'. A searcher may wish to locate references to the word in a table or Excel spreadsheet as a way of finding financial information, as rarely is the currency indicator used on internal budget spreadsheets. There may also be a need to index terms inside some specialized applications, such as Microsoft PowerPoint, Microsoft Visio and Microsoft Project.

Some search products go beyond this process of indexing, and undertake semantic analysis to identify words that are in fact the names of people and places; these are based on extensive dictionaries and linguistic rules.

In developing a specification for a search engine care needs to be taken to differentiate between the content acquisition schedule and the indexing schedule. It may well be that content is moved to the indexing server by a script, so that a document is moved as soon as it is added to the server. However, that content may only be indexed on a batch basis, perhaps overnight or at a weekend, so despite the rapid move of the document to the indexing server, the weakest link is the indexing schedule.

Another issue is the way in which the search engine indexes new content. Because of the need to rebuild the entire index, and the computer time that this involves, the search engine may only create a partial index of new content, perhaps on a daily basis, and then rebuild the indexes on a weekly basis.

The issues associated with indexing content in more than one language are discussed in Chapter 12.

Taxonomy management

A taxonomy is a hierarchical arrangement of entities in which there is a formal relationship (often referred to as a parent-child relationship) between every pair of terms. Taxonomies are very important in search applications. They enable a searcher to browse up and down a section of the hierarchy, looking for broader or narrower terms to provide a manageable list of search results. Definitions are often used in a colloquial sense and within a specific context. For instance, most people will know that a 'business school' is not related to the education of children but is a variant of a university or college. So the broader term might then be 'university'. Otherwise, broadening a search for courses on management might result in the search covering all types of schools from kindergarten upwards.

One of the most taxing areas for any organization is to decide on the level of effort that is put into taxonomy management. Although taxonomies can be created using computer software there will always need to be some human judgement on the results, and the issue is always about the balance between using software products and using information professionals with subject knowledge. A balance also has to be maintained between the effort involved in developing and maintaining a formal (even if limited in scope) taxonomy and using search technology to create taxonomy-like options on the fly.[2,3] Alan Gilchrist has provided a valuable summary of definitions of taxonomy and of the various types of taxonomic applications that are available.[4] These include:

- web directories, such as www.dmoz.com
- taxonomies to support automatic indexing
- taxonomies created by autocategorization tools, e.g. Gammasite (www.gammasite.com) and Verity K2 (www.autonomy.com)
- front-end filters to assist in managing search results
- corporate taxonomies that extend to all the content managed by the organization.

The resources needed to create a corporate taxonomy are immense. As an indication of the potential scale, GlaxoSmithKline has developed a taxonomy of 53,500 basic terms, 201,750 synonymns and 443,000 related terms.

However, the effectiveness of a search engine can be enhanced by developing taxonomies for specific types of content. In 2005 a small-scale survey carried out in the USA by Ron Daniel of Taxonomy Strategies LLC and Seth Earley of Earley & Associates gives a good indication of some of the approaches that are being used. The aim of the survey was to establish what might be current and emerging best practice (Table 2.1).

Stemming and lemmatization

Another important element of the indexing process is to undertake stemming, so that plurals and variants of words are identified. This is undertaken through a linguistic analysis that is appropriate for the language of the document. One of the leaders in the development of stemming algorithms is Martin Porter, who wrote the seminal stemming algorithm known as the Porter Stemming Algorithm.[5] Subsequently he developed Porter 2, also known as Snowball.[6] The websites for these two algorithms provide an excellent introduction to the basis of stemming and its value in information retrieval. However, stemming does not take the context of the word into account, and therefore cannot discriminate between words that have different meanings. Stemming also reduces the size of the index of a collection of documents.

A complementary approach is lemmatization, in which a word is reduced to its lemma, or basic element. This does require a knowledge of the language, and lemmatization tools are language dependent.

In some languages (those from Scandinavia and Finland are good examples), the language is highly inflected. For example, in Finnish several layers of endings may be affixed to word stems, indicating number, case, possession, modality, tense, person, and other morphological characteristics. This results in an enormous number of possible distinct word forms. A noun may have some 2000 forms, an adjective 6000, and a verb 12,000 forms.[7] There are also considerable problems with compound

Table 2.1 Results of a survey of taxonomy development approaches

	Not current practice	Being developed	In practice	Former practice	NA or unknown
'Org chart' taxonomy – one based primarily on the structure of the organization	36% (21)	10% (6)	34% (20)	5% (3)	15% (9)
'Products' taxonomy – one based primarily on the products and/or services offered by the organization	37% (22)	10% (6)	32% (19)	5% (3)	15% (9)
'Content types' taxonomy – one based primarily on the different types of document	28% (16)	21% (12)	40% (23)	5% (3)	7% (4)
'Topical' taxonomy – one based primarily on topics of interest to the site users	20% (12)	36% (21)	34% (20)	3% (2)	7% (4)
'Faceted' taxonomy – one that uses several of the approaches above	32% (19)	29% (17)	34% (20)	0% (0)	5% (3)
The taxonomy, or a portion of it, was licensed from an outside taxonomy vendor	75% (44)	3% (2)	14% (8)	0% (0)	8% (5)
The taxonomy follows a written 'style guide' to ensure its consistency over time	47% (28)	22% (13)	20% (12)	0% (0)	10% (6)
The taxonomy is maintained using a taxonomy editing tool other than MS Excel	35% (21)	17% (10)	40% (24)	2% (1)	7% (4)
The taxonomy was validated on a representative sample of content during its development	28% (17)	22% (13)	33% (20)	3% (2)	13% (8)
A roadmap for the future evolution of the taxonomy has been developed	38% (23)	40% (24)	13% (8)	0% (0)	8% (5)

nouns, as is the case in German, where there is no obvious point to assist a search engine to deconstruct the single word into its components.

Document confidentiality

On a public website all the content is also public. There may be some password-protected areas, but these can be clearly defined and the scope of the search managed appropriately. In the case of an intranet, and especially an enterprise search implementation, one of the constant challenges is to be able to manage the way in which confidential information is indexed. Where there is a drive or folder that is clearly designated as containing confidential information the problem is manageable. But that is rarely the case. All too often the circulation of a document is managed by e-mail, and no metadata is captured that will enable the circulation to be determined unambiguously from the document itself. There may also be a situation where some parts of a document (perhaps the main body of the text) have one level of security and the appendices a second level.

If there are any documents that have an element of restricted access these need to be identified at the outset of the specification of a search engine. It is essential that the organization have an agreed policy on document security from the outset, and that the effectiveness of procedures designed to ensure that only authorized staff are able to find specified documents is tested both from the start of the implementation and on a regular basis. The rules for access will be set out in access control lists (ACL), the computer industry term for a table defining the access a specific employee is allowed to a file or folder or other resource. Reaching agreement on these tends to be time-consuming and throw up various corporate culture and organizational issues.

One of the issues with ACLs is whether they run at the time the query is placed or are used to filter the results before presentation. The end result will be the same as regards the documents displayed to the user, but the implications for processing power and response times need to be considered. If the filtering is carried out on the results then there can be a perceptible time lag in displaying the hits, and this may either result in a call to the helpdesk commenting on the latency of the search feature, or alert the user to the fact that filtering is taking place.

The worst possible solution is to display the titles of content and then not permit the employee to open the documents, as not only could the title reveal the content, it could alert the user to the fact that they are not able to access certain information.

There are also some legal and regulatory issues to take into account. In the UK and many other countries there are export control regulations to prevent information about military equipment being sent to countries that might misuse such information. If the search engine indexes this content and perhaps summarizes it in the search results, this might be in breach of the regulations. Access to personal information under data protection legislation will also need to be considered (this is covered further in Chapter 6).

Query management

The next step is to match the user's query against the index. This is where there is a wide range of approaches, ranging from simply providing a means of entering keywords to the ability to find documents that are a close match to one that has already been deemed to be highly relevant. Evaluation of the best approach requires the organization to have a very good appreciation of how users will search for information and documents, and this is discussed in more detail in Chapter 7.

Many search engine vendors claim to offer natural language search queries. This statement needs to be considered carefully. Often it means that the search engine can accommodate the use of phrases such as 'the use of hash tables in information retrieval' and offer a range of options, from the all the words being present in a defined order down to any one of the words being present.

In addition, the query function should take care of some common problems. These include checking for spelling mistakes and offering alternatives, and ensuring that transliteration issues are addressed. This is to ensure that a search for Cologne also identifies content indexed as Köln.

Beyond this level an increasing number of semantic analysis techniques are now available that enable searches for gas production to exclude references to petroleum production in the USA, where gas is a synonym for petroleum.

Another technique is entity extraction, which involves identifying people, places and things, based on a combination of natural language processing and extensive dictionaries.

Ranking and relevance

Ranking and relevance are often used as synonyms, but they refer to different processes. The results of a search can be ranked by many different parameters, such as date, file type, language, and other metadata elements. The results can also be ranked by relevance, which is one of three ways of measuring the 'success' of a search. The other two are precision and recall.[8]

Recall and precision are mathematical measures of search performance that have a fixed range and are easy to compare across queries and engines.

> Recall = the number of relevant hits/number of relevant documents in the collection

Recall is 100% when every relevant document is retrieved. However, this implies that the number of relevant documents is known, which is very rarely the case except in situations where a search is being carried out (for example) to find the annual reports of the organization, which will be a known number.

> Precision = the number of relevant hits/the number of documents in the list

Precision is a measure of how well the engine performs in not retrieving irrelevant documents.

Arguably the greatest differentiating factor between search engines is how they compute a relevance ranking for the items retrieved against the query submitted by the searcher, as both the other measures involve a definition of relevance.

Web search engines give reasonably good recall but poor precision, i.e. they find some relevant documents, but they also provide too many non-relevant hits that users do not want to read. An enterprise search engine must have a high recall to be admissible in most applications. The problem for vendors is how to increase precision without sacrificing recall. To increase recall typically introduces more bad hits into the hit list, thereby reducing precision, whereas trying to increase precision typically reduces recall by removing some good hits from the list.

One of the major advances in determining the relevance of a document was the development in 1972 of the concept of term specificity (later called inverse document frequency, IDF) by Karen Spärck Jones. The premise, which has since been tested by many research groups, is that a query term that appears in only a few documents in a collection should be given more weight than one that appears in a large number of documents. This is based on a heuristic principle, and much of the research work on IDF has focused on proving the heuristic from first principles.[9,10]

Another important advance in text retrieval was the development of a relevance weighting model by Stephen Robertson and Karen Spärck-Jones, working at The City University in London, and later at the Microsoft Research Centre at the University of Cambridge. This is often referred to as RSJ, after the surnames of the authors.

Both IDF and RSJ focus on the weighting of terms in a collection of documents. The next step was to incorporate a weighting of the number of terms in a specific document, defined as the term frequency. It was largely the work of Gerald Salton and his team at Cornell University that brought together the concepts of term frequency and inverse document frequency to form the TD*IDF relevance formulation, which is the basis of relevance ranking in most search engines.

A great deal of research work has been carried out on ranking algorithms, much of it in the UK led by the Centre for Interactive Systems Research (CISR) at The City University. This was formed in 1987, with the aim of bringing together a group working on various aspects of information retrieval.

The most prominent result of this work was the ranking algorithm known as Okapi BM25 (Best Match - the origin of the 25 is unknown), in which TD*IDF is a major component. BM25 also includes a parameter which reflects the fact that a short document containing a given number of keywords is likely to be of greater relevance than a longer document with the same number of keywords.

Vector space model

One of the core elements of the search software developed by Autonomy Corporation is the use of the vector space model, developed at Cornell

University in the late 1960s and initially used in the SMART Information Retrieval System. The leader of the project was Gerald Salton, who was Professor of Computer Science at Cornell and is one of the acknowledged innovators in information retrieval.

In outline, in a vector space model each term and each document in which those terms are found is calculated as a vector, using a formula in which the components are the frequency with which the term occurred in the document, the number of documents containing the term, and the total number of documents in the set. Relevance rankings are then calculated based on how large the deviation of the angles are for each document vector in relation to the original query vector.

Meaning-based computing

Over the last two decades there has been a great deal of research on semantic analysis and natural language query processing. A prominent proponent of this approach has been Mike Lynch, the CEO of Autonomy Corporation. The Autonomy IDOL server makes use of the Bayesian statistical inference theory (named after Thomas Bayes) and Claude Shannon's seminal work on information theory and information entropy. The overall aim has been to identify concepts (e.g. innovation) that are not explicitly stated or indexable from the document. As well as providing search functionality to text documents, the principles can be extended to static and video image retrieval.

An increasing number of commercial search software vendors are offering semantic analysis and related technologies, and this will be an important development route in the coming years. Two approaches that have been used are latent semantic analysis,[11] which was developed in 1988 by Scott Deerwester and his colleagues, and probabilistic latent semantic analysis,[12] which was developed by Thomas Hofmann and is used in the Recommind search software.

There is much debate over the benefits of the various approaches that have been developed for relevance determination. There is no 'best' approach and much depends on the characteristics of the content being searched and the types of query being used. This is why it is of the greatest importance in search engine selection to carry out evaluations on representative test files of the content.

Manipulating relevance algorithms

Many search engine vendors make a point of enabling search administrators to modify relevance ranking to force certain words or concepts to have a greater weight (given the context of the objectives of the organization) than might be the case in a 'neutral' situation.

Ranking can also be 'turned off' for certain queries to provide a manually generated 'best bets' option. For example, an organization may decide that any search for information on a specific product always returns the corporate marketing strategy for that product as the first hit. This is sometimes referred to as static ranking, but needs to be used with care. The fact that a document has had its ranking forced in this way needs to be obvious from the search page, and in addition only a very few documents for any given search term should be given a static ranking.

Results formatting

The critical issue with results formatting is to present users with an initial list of results that enable them to refine the search with a high degree of confidence that they are 'going in the right direction'. There is nothing more frustrating than to do further work on a set of results and find that in fact the original set was not as relevant as at first seemed to be the case. The extent to which the display format for results can be customized is one of the key differentiating factors between search engines. This subject is covered in more detail in Chapter 7.

Another issue that needs to be considered under this heading is the way in which duplicate documents are handled. Users do not want to see multiple references to the corporate strategy held on each of a dozen different national intranets in a major corporation. However, are these documents actually the same, or are only the title and some core text the same, but in addition there is a country-specific section that is of considerable importance to the searcher? This is where a full understanding of the document collection is fundamentally important in deciding whether the way in which a specific search product handles de-duplication is relevant to the needs of the organization.

The extent of de-duplication and other actions that the search software is taking in managing the selection of hits to present will also have an impact on search performance.

Document access

Identifying the existence of relevant documents is only the first of two important steps. As mentioned above, the search engine is searching through an index of documents, not the document itself. When the user needs to read or print out the document the server then needs to point to the server on which the document currently resides. This may be a different server from the one on which the document was originally posted, or of course the document itself may now have been deleted from the server. The process is sometimes referred to as 'rendering' a document.

Some search vendors generate an HTML file from the document so that only a 'light' version of the file is retrieved for inspection. This is the approach used by Google in offering an HTML version of a PDF file. This will not have any pagination, and if search terms are highlighted then the only way to see all the occurrences is to scroll through the HTML file, as there is no way to page through it sequentially.

Another approach is to have a repository for the search engine where all documents that have been indexed are maintained. This will enhance the speed with which documents are presented to the user, but the problem of ensuring that the document does still exist through synchronization with the original document still remains. There is also the issue of each document being stored twice, creating a considerable increase in storage requirements.

One feature that can put a considerable strain on document access is where sections of the document containing a specific keyword or phrase are presented sequentially to the user. Each occurrence has to be retrieved either from the document repository or from the server on which the document resides, and this has some significant processing issues.

Comparative evaluation of search software

The complexity of search software is such that considerable care needs to be taken when assessing its merits and those of search appliances. The differences between vendors are often quite subtle, and given the highly competitive nature of the industry few will disclose any detail about the way in which their software works. The only reliable way to assess the benefits of a specific approach to the elements of the search process is to test them on a specific group of documents. The selection of such a group of documents is discussed in Chapter 5.

One of the main forums for the discussion and evaluation of search technologies is the Text REtrieval Conference (TREC), co-sponsored by the National Institute of Standards and Technology (NIST) and the US Department of Defense and begun in 1992. The objective of TREC[13] is to support research within the information retrieval community by providing the infrastructure necessary for large-scale evaluation of text retrieval methodologies.

The TREC workshop series has the following goals:

- to encourage research in information retrieval based on large test collections
- to increase communication among industry, academia and government by creating an open forum for the exchange of research ideas
- to speed the transfer of technology from research laboratories into commercial products by demonstrating substantial improvements in retrieval methodologies on real-world problems
- to increase the availability of appropriate evaluation techniques for use by industry and academia, including the development of new evaluation techniques more applicable to current systems.

The TREC programme consists of a number of tracks, for which there is a standard set of documents and tasks against which academic research teams and commercial search vendors can test out elements of their methodology.

For each TREC track, NIST provides a test set of documents and questions. Participants run their own retrieval systems on the data, and return to NIST a list of the retrieved top-ranked documents. NIST pools the individual results, judges the retrieved documents for correctness, and evaluates the results. The TREC cycle ends with a workshop that is a forum for participants to share their experiences.

The proceedings of the TREC conferences (which generally take place in November each year, but are restricted to participating organizations) are published on the TREC website, and typically there are around 100 papers.

Text mining

Text mining and search are complementary technologies. The object of searching is to find specific information to meet a defined requirement. Text mining[14] is on a much larger scale, working through perhaps hundreds of thousands of documents to identify trends and patterns using sophisticated language-specific algorithms. The techniques of text mining fall outside the scope of this book but the technology will become increasngly important over the next few years. CMS Watch is publishing a report on text mining products in early 2007.

References

1 Langville, A. N., and Meyer, C. D. (2006) *Google's PageRank and Beyond - the science of search engine rankings*, Princeton NJ, Princeton University Press.

2 Fledman, S. (2004) Why Categorize? *KMWorld*, (October), 8-10, www.kmworld.com.

3 Wyllie, J. (2005) *Taxonomy Frameworks for Corporate Knowledge*, 2nd edn, Ark Group, www.ark-group.com.

4 Gilchrist, A. (2005) Thesauri, Taxonomies and Ontologies - an etymological approach, *Journal of Documentation*, **59** (1), 7-18.

5 www.tartarus.org/~martin/PorterStemmer/index.html.

6 http://snowball.tartarus.org/texts/introduction.html.

7 Korenius, T., Lauikkala, J., Jarvelin, K. and Juhola M. (2004) *Stemming and Lemmatization in the Clustering of Finnish Text Documents*, www.info.uta.fi/tutkimus/fire/archive/KLJJ-CIKM04.pdf.

8 Mavesh, K. (2006) *Text Retrieval Quality: a primer*, www.oracle.com/technology/products/text/htdocs/imt_quality.htm.

9 Robertson, S. E. and Spärck Jones, K. (1994) Simple Proven Approaches to Text Retrieval, University of Cambridge Computer Laboratory Technical Report UCAM-CL-TR-346, www.cl/cam.ac.uk/TechReports/UCAM-CL-TR-356.

10 Robertson, S. (2004) Understanding Inverse Document Frequency: on theoretical arguments for IDF, *Journal of Documentation*, **60** (5), 503–20.

11 http://en.wikipedia.org/wiki/Latent_semantic_indexing.

12 http://en.wikipedia.org/wiki/Probabilistic_latent_semantic_analysis.

13 http://trec.nist.gov/overview.html.

14 Feldman, R. and Sanger, J. (2006) *The Text Mining Handbook: advanced approaches in analyzing unstructured data*, Cambridge, Cambridge University Press.

Chapter 3

The search business

In this chapter:

- How big is the search market?
- The impact of Google, Microsoft and IBM
- What is a search appliance?
- The benefits of a hosted search application
- Profiles of over 50 search vendors

The market for search

The challenge for the software industry is to develop robust and effective software products based on the principles set out in Chapter 2. Until the launch of the CMS Watch Enterprise Search Report[1] the search business was very poorly documented and understood, unless the organization subscribed to services from companies such as Gartner, IDC and Forrester. The Enterprise Search Report was written by Steve Arnold and contains detailed evaluations of around 30 search products. The level of detail in the report, both on the basic technology of search and in the features of the main search engine applications, is substantial and is essential reading.

The search business is very fragmented, and compared to other software markets not very large in sales of standalone search products. In March

2006 the Gartner Group estimated that sales of new search software licences would total just under $370 million. The total revenues of the search software vendors is probably around twice this amount thanks to the support, maintenance and upgrade fees charged to existing customers, so that the total market value is perhaps around $700 million. Autonomy (including revenues from Verity) probably accounts for around 45% of this revenue, and Fast Search and Google for a further 20%. These figures can be no more than estimates, as many of the companies profiled below are privately owned and disclose little or no financial information. For example, one major search vendor announced in November 2006 that it had a 109% year-on-year revenue growth in the third quarter. This is certainly impressive, but no mention was made about the profitability of the company.

Over the last couple of years there have been some acquisitions in the industry, but only the Autonomy/Verity deal involved two quoted companies. Triple Hop was acquired by Oracle in September 2005, and a couple of months later IBM bought iPhrase, in both cases for undisclosed amounts.

The search industry is much more than a collection of independent software vendors, as all the major IT companies offer search products, notably IBM (which offers its Websphere OmniFind product on AIX, Linux, Solaris and Windows platforms), Oracle and SAP. In addition, the leading document management/enterprise content management vendors include powerful search functionality, developed either as an integral component of a document management suite (such as OpenText/Hummingbird) or as a closely integrated third-party product, as is the case with ECM Documentum and Fast Search. Alfresco, the open source ECM vendor, appropriately includes Lucene, the only major open source enterprise search software. There are a number of open source search software products for websites, notably ht://Dig.

The major IT industry consultancies differ in their view of the constituent companies in the search market. Forrester Research Inc., in its Q2 2006 report on Enterprise Search Platforms, compared only Autonomy, Convera, Endeca, Entopia, Fast Search, Google, IBM and Microsoft. Gartner, on the other hand, profiled 26 companies in its 2005 Magic Quadrant for

Information Access Technologies. That is not to say that the Forrester report is incomplete or misleading, but to emphasize that these reports need to be read through for their definitions and comparison methodology, and not just for the charts that are often cited by search vendors in their publicity material.

Search appliances

There are two other sectors of the search business. The first of these is the search appliance business, which was started by Thunderstone but is now dominated by Google, with its range of search appliances. A search appliance bundles hardware (processing power and storage for the indexes) together with the search software itself. The resulting box is designed to be shipped direct to the customer and then installed in standard server racks. Implementation times are very short, typically an hour or so.

Generally these products are priced on the basis of the number of documents indexed. In the case of Google, when the Google search appliance (GSA) reaches the document limit it keeps crawling. There is a 20% buffer allotted for content above the limit that it fills up. Once the buffer is full, the GSA begins to drop out the least relevant content from the index to bring the document count back down to the licence limit.

Hosted search

One of the interesting developments in the search business is the growth of outsourced search services. These services are designed primarily to provide search functionality for websites, especially for customers who have limited internal IT resources but to whom a resilient and powerful search feature on their website is important. Among the companies offering hosted search are (see Appendix for details):

- Blossom Software
- CrownPeak
- Fast Search
- Funnelback
- Innerprise

- Mondosoft
- WebSideStory (through the acquisition of Atomz).

The use of outsourced searching still seems to be in its infancy in Europe, despite the fact that both Fast Search (Norway) and Mondosoft (Denmark) offer this service.

Google

Google has transformed the level of awareness about the value of enterprise search through the aggressive marketing of its search appliances. Almost since the launch of Google as a public search site many senior managers have wanted their enterprise search to work like Google. The problem was (and is) that the way Google is able to offer web search functionality and relevance ranking does not apply inside the enterprise. The search appliance product was first announced in 2002 and started shipping in volume in 2004. The current release is Version 4, and the rate of product development has been very high.

This is likely to continue. Google undoubtedly has a long-term vision for the enterprise search market, and the current generation of products are only at the market entry level. In order to manage its web search service, Google is probably carrying out more research and development in database design and information retrieval than any other software company and the outcomes of this effort will become steadily more visible over the next few years.

The Google Mini is designed for the needs of small and medium-sized deployments. The Mini provides a search solution for web-enabled content and content in file systems with up to 300,000 documents (or unique URLs). The entry-level Mini searches up to 50,000 documents for $1995, which includes a one-year support contract. Additional versions search up to 100,000, 200,000 or 300,000 documents. Currently there is no trial version of the Mini, although Google does offer a 30-day money-back deal.

The Google search appliance is designed for larger businesses and can support up to 30 million documents. It also includes a variety of unique features, such as:

- access control for secure content
- support for content from relational databases
- direct integration with content management systems
- support for third-party content feeds
- automated query expansion (context-sensitive stemming, automated synonym creation).

Google originally anticipated that both products would be 'plug and play', but rather underestimated the level of expertise in even large organizations. The company has now set up a global network of partners that will support the installation and implementation of the products, primarily the search appliance.

However, the level of expertise in both Google technology and the use of search within an organization should be checked before selecting an integration partner, of which there are a number in most European countries. Partners for Australia and New Zealand were not announced until late 2006, and there are still countries where partner integrators have yet to be announced, such as Norway and Finland, and most of the new EU Member States.

In 2005 Google launched OneBox, which enables the Google search appliance to interface with specialized database applications from companies that initially included Cisco, Cognos, Employease, Netsuite, Oracle, Salesforce.com and SAS. The OneBox module (which can be modified for specific applications through a range of APIs) only undertakes a search of the specific database application when certain trigger keywords are included in the query made to the search appliance. The results from the database application are then posted at the top of the results page, and currently up to four different OneBox modules can be integrated into the search process.

Currently Google provides helpdesk support through e-mail: there is no telephone access to technical support staff. It is therefore important to be clear about what support is being provided by the local integrator and what support will be provided directly by Google.

There is a Google Enterprise Blog[2] which has links to discussion groups for the Google Mini and the Google search appliance.

IBM

IBM has a long history of involvement in both information retrieval research and the development of search software. In 1962 IBM developed the PRIME (Planning through Retrieval of Information for Management) software, which could search through the records of documents and used both Boolean logic and word proximity functionality. However, IBM is probably most famous for the development of STAIRS (Storage and Retrieval System) as a multi-user timeshare product which was launched in 1970. One of the catalysts for much of the early work on full-text retrieval by IBM was the antitrust suit filed by Control Data Corporation in 1968. This led to the development of TEXT-PAC to create an index to 25 million pages of internal documentation. Further development led to the AQUARIUS software, which was used in connection with a number of other antitrust suits, and this was then commercialized by IBM in 1970 as STAIRS. Support for this was only discontinued in 1994, which is a long time in software development and support terms, and says much for the quality of the original design.

The company has a large information retrieval research group based in the IBM Research Laboratories in Haifa, Israel,[3] and there is an information management research group at the Almaden Research Laboratories in California. There is also an Intelligent Information Management Department at the IBM T. J. Watson Research Center which is addressing technical challenges in database systems and information management. The department includes the Database Research Group and the Intelligent Information Analysis Group. The Intelligent Information Analysis Group Group is developing a new multimedia analysis and retrieval system called MARVEL. The objectives behind MARVEL are to organize the large and growing amounts of multimedia data such video, images and audio by using machine learning techniques to automatically add metadata to this type of content.

The primary search product of IBM at present is Omnifind, which is a component of the Websphere Information Integration platform. This is based on IBM's unstructured information management architecture (UIMA),[4] which supports the creation, discovery, composition and deployment of a broad range of analysis capabilities and the linking of them to structured information services, such as databases or search engines. The objective of the UIMA framework is to offer an environment where other search vendors can plug in and run their UIMA component implementations.

In 2005 IBM acquired iPhrase, a company with some highly innovative approaches to search, and these have now been incorporated into the IBM WebSphere Content Discovery Server. In December 2006 IBM and Yahoo! jointly announced the IBM OmniFind Yahoo! Edition as an enterprise search application which can be downloaded free of charge, where there are no more than 500,000 documents to search. However what is being offered is not OmniFind itself but Lucene, one of the few open-source enterprise search applications. What seems to be the plan of both IBM and Google is to use their search solutions as a Trojan Horse marketing solution to get inside an organization and then sell up and across. From an IBM perspective every download of its new product is a qualified sales lead. Google itself has not been standing still, and in early January announced some important enhancements to the search functionality of the Enterprise Search Appliance products relating to results hit clustering, source biasing and open source connectors for indexing content in SharePoint 2003 and SharePoint 2007.

Microsoft

Although Microsoft has been a major player in the public web search business it has not been at the forefront of enterprise search, even though the company has been at the centre of information retrieval research for many years with the Information Retrieval Centre at the Microsoft Research Centre in Cambridge, UK.[5] Of the major IT vendors, this commitment is matched only by IBM. In particular, the search implementation on the current (2003) version of Microsoft SharePoint has been poor.

SharePoint 2007 was released at the end of 2006, but the first service pack was due to be released in March 2007, which suggests that there are still some bugs in the software. The extent to which users of SharePoint Portal 2003 will migrate to the 2007 version is not yet clear, and one of the issues that will have to be taken into account is file migration.

As far as the search functionality is concerned, among the major enhancements and additional features are:

- Office SharePoint Server 2007 and Windows SharePoint Services now use a common implementation of Microsoft Search.
- There is a much enhanced relevance engine, including support for Best Bets keyword searching.
- The search engine can be extended to search content repositories outside of SharePoint itself, for example data in a client relationship management system.
- Centralized management of indexing and search across multiple SharePoint servers.
- Inbuilt search logging.

However, in effect this is not an upgraded version of the search functionality of SharePoint 2003 but a total rebuild, and as such SharePoint 2007 will now be a significant competitive threat to other search software companies.

Oracle

Oracle has never been a major player in search because its products were always bundled into an enterprise licence. Late in 2006 Oracle announced that it was releasing Secure Enterprise Search 10g as a standalone product. The title of the product is important to note, because one of the core features is the security management features. These rely on other Oracle applications being installed, and without these the product is very similar to other enterprise search products in terms of the scale of the document repositories and search use that it can manage.

SAP

SAP has provided enterprise text search for users of SAP portal technology for some time, but has restricted the search functionality to content held in the SAP repository. In 2007 SAP will expand the search capability of its NetWeaver product to search data and text repositories throughout the enterprise.

Other search software vendors

A directory of search engine vendors is given in the Appendix.

References

1 *Enterprise Search Report*, Washington DC, CMS Watch, www.cmswatch.com.
2 http://googleenterprise.blogspot.com/.
3 www.research.ibm.com/haifa/dept/imt/ir.html.
4 http://domino.research.ibm.com/comm/research.nsf/pages/r.nlp.innovation.html.
5 http://research.microsoft.com/research/ir/.

Chapter 4

Making a business case for search

In this chapter:

- What are the hardware, software and staff requirements?
- Understanding total cost of implementation
- Using risk management to make a business case

Introduction

It is not easy to build a business case for investing in search applications. The benefits of a search engine are very difficult to measure, even though there is good evidence from surveys that searching for information is time-consuming and often frustrating. In the case of content management software applications often relatively standard processes are being undertaken on a regular basis. Search is not like that. Implementing a search engine may reduce the time spent on searching for information, but in most organizations that is not a measurable quantity. As with most productivity tools, is the time freed up then used for other tasks, or is it still used for searching but now over a wider range of documents and with increasing care being taken to find the most relevant?

When implementing content management software, many companies have found that the costs of professional support from the vendor or systems integrator are considerably more than the base licence cost. However, once the implementation has been accomplished the staff costs associated with maintaining the software are quite low. This is not the case with search software, where there will be a continual requirement to optimize its performance.

This is also the hidden cost of using open source software. Although the use of open source software is still very low in enterprise applications, there are many open source products that can be used for website searching, where in many respects the requirements are less demanding.

One of the standard approaches to justifying investment in software is a return on investment (ROI) analysis. Generally speaking, only in the professional services sector is time logged and costed on a sufficiently normalized basis for a case to be made about the impact of productivity tools. Even then, trying to build a business case that will satisfy an accountant is a major challenge.

Chapters 9 and 10 cover some of the issues that need to be considered when making a business case for investment in search for a website and for an intranet, but this chapter sets out some generic issues about the development of a business case.

Total cost of implementation

The first step is to be clear about what factors will affect the cost of a search implementation. In developing the business plan it is important to take account of the total cost of implementation over at least a three-year period. The cost elements of implementing a search engine are quite diverse, and include the following.

Licence fee

The formula for the core licence varies between vendors. It could be based on:

- the number of documents (common with search appliances)
- the number of users
- the number of concurrent users
- the number of searches

- the total file size of the content to be indexed
- the number of servers needed to run the search software.

This makes comparisons between vendors difficult, and also makes it difficult to carry out any comparative ROI assessment across a number of vendors.

If there is no current search function then estimating the number of searches that will be made is impossible, and yet that is what some vendors ask for, mainly because they are concerned about hardware requirements.

The licence structure for the Google search appliance is rather different from that of a traditional software licence. The Google search appliance website makes the following statement:

> The Google Search Appliance is sold as a two-year licence, with hardware, software, product updates, support and product replacement coverage all included for one low price.

Because a search engine would typically be installed and maintained for at least three years, when comparing the costs of the Google product against a search software product it is important to develop a three-year total cost of ownership model.

Software maintenance and helpdesk support

This will typically be 15–20% per year, and is usually for maintenance of the current version of the software. Most vendors start the maintenance contract on the date of installation of the software, thus increasing the Year 1 cost by 20%. It is important to look at what services are provided under the maintenance agreement, especially in terms of on-site assistance.

One factor to be taken into consideration is helpdesk support. Search software often works on a global basis, and there may need to be support for a number of sites around the world. This may result in some additional costs in having access to more than one helpdesk location. The search solution may also have been installed and supported locally by a systems integrator (as is the case with the Google search appliance), and it is important to determine what queries will be handled locally and which will be passed to the vendor for a response.

Upgrades

There will almost certainly be a charge for upgrades to the search engine. Bug fixes and other minor changes to the software will be included in the software maintenance fee, but major upgrades will almost certainly be charged for. Such major upgrades may well result in the need for further training of the technical and search support teams, and may have knock-on effects on other elements of the search platform, such as file space.

Additional modules

The larger vendors offer a range of add-on modules (such as optical character recognition software to index scanned documents) that may not be required for smaller collections of documents, or for the initial stage of the roll-out. Quantifying the likely cost of these at some point in the future is important, but not easy to accomplish.

Additional licences

There may be a requirement to purchase additional licences (often referred to as instances) for the search servers if the scale of the indexes requires them to be split across two servers for failsafe operation.

Professional services

The search engine vendor will almost certainly be involved in the initial implementation, including either writing or verifying the content acquition scripts and crawlers, and ensuring that the technical configuration of the search engine is correct. The extent of any further professional services support from the vendor depends on the design of the software and the extent of in-house development skills. The situation inevitably becomes more complex where a systems integrator has provided the implementation support.

In the case of content management software professional services, the costs range from a factor of 1 for a low-end system to a factor of 4 for an enterprise implementation. The factors for search are not dissimilar. One of the factors that will affect the level of professional services is the extent to which the organization itself is able to undertake the implementation. Rates for skilled staff can be of the order of $2000 a day.

Hardware and network enhancement

There may well be a need for new server hardware and for additional storage. Most IT departments will be unfamiliar with the requirements of a full-text search engine and may well underestimate them. The index to a set of documents can take up perhaps 50% of the space of the original documents, although many vendors are now working to reduce this amount by stemming and compression techniques. There may need to be load balancing, and if the search engine is to provide 24/7 levels of service then the redundancy requirements must be quantified. Bandwidth that provides adequate levels of document presentation may require some upgrading of the network.

In a distributed file server environment there may be a requirement to index remotely, and the network capacity to support both this and the subsequent downloading of documents needs to be taken into account.

Training

Training will not be required only at the time of implementation, but also as new content servers , or new features are added to the search scope. Although it is probably an oversimplification of the situation, if there is a major requirement for user training then the search application is arguably too complex for the purpose to which it is being put.

Some search engine vendors offer a 'train-the-trainer' approach. In theory this is an excellent idea, but often the person chosen to go on the course is a 'power user' who does not have the skills to train others. In such situations the ability to train should be a determining factor as to the choice of staff who attend such a course.

Training needs become steadily more complex in multinational or even national but multiple site implementations. Although many vendors offer in-context help screens, these may not be available in all the languages of the countries that have access to the search system.

In-house support team

Organizations invariably fail to appreciate the staff resources that are going to be required to support an enterprise search application, not just on the IT support and application development side, but also on the development of taxonomies, classifications, best bets, synonyms, and a host of other ongoing search enhancement issues. Even an intranet search implementation will require at least one member of staff whose main task is to work through the search logs and other feedback to optimize the search performance. In the case of a large enterprise search implementation the team could be as many as five people. The support requirements will be different in the case of an open source product such as Lucene, as the support team will need to have good development skills.

Search analytics

The capabilities of the search log analytics provided by vendors vary widely. In the case of intranet and enterprise implementations the logs can be complex to unravel, and yet the ability to drill down into some specific search problems is essential. The need to purchase additional analytics software should be assessed at the procurement stage and taken into account in developing the budget.

Price-performance

One of the difficulties in making a business case for search in an enterprise situation is that there is no simple relationship between the functionality offered by the search software and the licence cost of the product. It is also very difficult to anticipate the hardware and network costs that might be involved, because the performance of the search engine cannot easily be modelled in advance of implementation.

The situation is substantially easier for web search, especially if the hosted-search route is chosen, but in general file sizes will be much smaller, and because the rate of change of content will be less, indexing will require less processing power and time.

Making a business case

Attempts to make a business case based on ROI or productivity improvements are likely to result in a set of figures that is almost impossible to defend, especially in an intranet situation. As mentioned in Chapter 1, some research has been done on the amount of time people spend searching for information. In principle, it might be argued that adding a search engine to an intranet, or enhancing the current search engine, would mean that employees will spend less time searching, leading to a measurable improvement in productivity.

One case study of the scale of the problems faced by large organizations was presented by John Birchak and Luke Koons of Intel, in a paper to the 2006 Enterprise Search Summit. Intel carries out a range of studies on information-seeking behaviours and some of the metrics reported were:

- The average employee wastes 10% of their time searching for information.
- Product planners and design engineers waste 30% of their time searching.
- 87% of respondents had to duplicate content that existed but could not be found, with the average time wasted being around nine hours.
- 38% reported project delays due to missing content.
- 70% have to revise their search query three times or more to find out what they need.

This type of information collection and analysis is beyond the scope of most organizations, but even a few case studies can be very telling.

Another approach is to develop a risk profile of the organization with regard to ability to access information. Some typical risks that might make the case for an intranet or enterprise search engine are:

- not being able to respond to a request for a document from a regulatory authority
- not being able to find documents in connection with legal proceedings
- not being able to quote a competitive price on a project because documents that contained organizational knowledge could not be found

- not being able to locate information needed to develop reliable business plans and strategies
- having to duplicate work because the original documents could not be found
- not being able to find documents that contained out-of-date or erroneous information in order to remove them from the servers
- not being able to respond quickly to requests from customers and clients for information they would expect the organization to have immediate access to
- making decisions based only on erroneous internal information, because the latest information from external sources cannot be integrated with internal information
- Not being able to identify expertise in the organization because documents that might indicate those with that expertise could not be found.

These are indicative, and there are many more instances where an inability to locate information will put the organization at risk.

The situation is somewhat easier with a website because the search logs will show that the amount and character of the traffic has improved, and that more transactions are being carried out.

Chapter 5

Specifying and selecting a search engine

In this chapter:

- Using personas to develop a specification
- The critical role that a document audit plays in search selection
- IT systems architecture issues
- The stages of the selection process

Introduction

The basic principles of specifying and selecting search software are the same as for any other category of software, including a clear identification of the business need, and defining user requirements. However, with search software the process of defining user requirements is more complex, because:

- There is a range of tasks that the search software will be supporting.
- There is unlikely to be any previous experience of specifying search software.
- Specifying the performance of search software involves both hardware-related elements (which are relatively easy to specify) and user-related elements that are much more difficult to specify.

- The performance will be highly specific to a specific collection, or collections, of documents.

Indeed, where there is currently no search feature, or at best very limited search functionality, there can be some substantial issues in developing a specification against which to evaluate the search products. For example, at least one search vendor requires information about the number of searches to be conducted in order to scale the hardware for the system.

Using personas to specify user requirements

The use of personas to specify user requirements for websites and intranets is now well established, and there is a considerable literature on how to undertake persona development.[1-5]

A persona is a real virtual user. The 'person' described does not actually exist, but is created through research to typify some of the characteristics of a group of users. Biographical details are developed, even down to a photograph, so that the persona is so 'real' that the web team or intranet team start to identify with them as individual members of staff or as visitors to the website.

The main characteristics of personas are as follows:

- Personas are hypothetical archetypes, or 'stand-ins' for actual users, that assist in defining and prioritizing user requirements.
- Personas are not real people, but represent real people throughout the specification process, and are defined in sufficient detail to create the illusion that they are real people.
- Personas are defined by the tasks they undertake, not by the organizational structure.
- Personas are not an end in themselves, but are used to develop scenarios that illustrate how they carry out their tasks to achieve organizational objectives. The scenarios can then be used for usability and performance evaluations of pilot and operational versions of the search engine.

Determine initial user segmentation

This should be done by taking an initial high-level view of the organization. As a fictional example for the purposes of illustration, take the case of a European pharmaceutical company. The research base is in France, along with administration, sales and marketing for continental Europe. Manufacturing is carried out in Germany, Spain and Croatia, and there is a significant UK office to support sales, marketing and medical information. As well as an intranet there is a customer management system and a document management system, as well as a number of specialized databases developed by the IT department.

An initial review of the organization's structure might arrive at the following core groups:

- research scientists working on new drug formulations, needing access to highly confidential internal documents and also to external databases, as well as wishing to carry out chemical substructure searches
- clinical trials teams working through the drug registration process, again involving highly confidential information, much of it in a numeric format that may require range searching
- medical information specialists dealing with enquiries from doctors and pharmacists about the correct use of the drugs, or initially reporting on adverse reactions. Speed of response is essential to deal with these enquiries
- product development teams working on formulations and product packaging, which may need to look at images of packing, and need to be aware of what is happening in the marketplace
- sales and marketing teams looking for information on sales channels, sales reports, and the activities of competitors. Again, there may be some urgency to track down this information
- administration and support staff looking for policy and procedure documents. Unlike those used by the groups above, these documents will almost certainly be in all the local languages where the company has operations.

Conduct focus groups

The purpose of constructing these groups is to begin to determine the way in which the members of each group search for documents. The emphasis should be on identifying tasks that might require use to be made of a search engine, and some ways in which the queries might be framed. Staff using external online search services, such as Medline, will probably have a better idea than others about the types of search undertaken.

Define scenarios

The development of a set of personas is not an end in itself. Personas are taken as the basis for a set of scenarios, and there may be more than one scenario for each persona. These scenarios can then be used in the request for a proposal (RFP) to define search requirements, and also form the basis of usability tests later in the implementation process.

Document audit

Much useful work on the nature of enterprise documents may have been carried out in the specification of a content management system (CMS), but the focus and level of detail are different for a search engine. The work carried out for a CMS tends to focus on document types and workflow issues. Document-type information is useful in specifying a search engine, but there are many more elements of the collections to determine.

These include the following:

1. How many documents will need to be indexed? At a minimum the file size for each of the repositories has to be defined, but in addition the number of documents also needs to be determined to obtain a reliable estimate of the licence cost. The count does not need to go to the nearest document, but certainly needs to be within 10% of the actual number.
2. In the case of e-mails the text element is much shorter than a standard office document. A rule of thumb would be to divide the number of e-mails by five to get an equivalent document count.
3. What is the categorization of documents by size/word count? In an enterprise situation there might be documents that total several

hundred pages. This is important to know, because it may be necessary to specify the capabilities of any automated summarization capability in the search software, or assess the way in which query terms will be displayed in the context of the document.

4. What file types are in use? There are likely to be more than just the familiar Microsoft Office file formats, especially if there are document and client management applications that need to be searched.
5. How important is it to be able to tag and index images, tables and other non-linear text?
6. On what servers are those documents held, and what other files are on the server that might have an impact on defining what content is to be indexed?
7. What security and confidentiality issues need to be taken into consideration?
8. Are there any taxonomies, controlled term lists or classification schemes that need to be taken into account?
9. What languages are in use? Are all documents in a single language, or do some have a mixture of languages?
10. How many documents are translations, so that a search could be carried out in one language and then the document pointed to?
11. What might be some of the high-frequency terms used in the document where it would be essential to be able to add in qualifiers to reduce the number of documents retrieved to an acceptable level?
12. What is the rate of creation of new documents, and over what period (hours, days, weeks)? This needs to be determined with a reasonable degree of precision, because it will point to the need for different index crawl periodicities. This will not add to the cost of the search software, but the ability to manage these crawl periodicities will need to be established.
13. How time-critical is it for certain categories of document to be indexed and searchable within a given period after they have been added to the system (minutes, hours, days)?
14. How much manual tagging has to be carried out on specific types of document, and what delay might this introduce into the system?
15. How valuable would it be to develop a 'best bets' approach, and

what is the scale of resource required to accomplish this to support whatever functionality is provided by the search software?

16 What searches are currently carried out on external online/web services that may need to be integrated into the enterprise search?

The questions are fairly simple, but the research to obtain the information required is likely to be quite time-consuming. One reason for this is that the questions must be answered in the light not only of the characteristics of the current collection of documents, but of how the enterprise search engine may be extended to other collections over the next few years. Forward planning is essential in specifying a search engine.

With website search the situation is usually more straightforward, but this does not mean that the document (or rather content) audit can be ignored.

One essential outcome of this work is to define a collection of documents that can be used as a test file in evaluating a search engine, and in the initial implementation to check that all the servers are functioning according to specification. The size of the test file cannot be specified on the basis of a percentage of the total document collection, and it may be that there is more than one test file.

Ideally there should be three test collections:

1 A few documents from every one of the current and projected file types to check how the search engine will handle these file types. Microsoft Project can be one common file format that cannot be searched, and the way in which Excel files with multiple workbooks are handled is another area for evaluation.

2 A large set of typical documents that will be a prime collection for searching by the persona types developed in the business case. This could be human resources policies, engineering reports or business plans.

3 If appropriate, a smaller set of very large documents to test out summarization and keyword-in-context functionalities.

This collection needs to be developed for all the languages that will be supported by the search engine. Whether or not these test files need to be provided to the search vendor as a CD depends on the availability of a download of the search software for evaluation purposes.

However, just creating a test file is only part of the requirement. The objective is to test retrieval performance, and so a test set of questions, derived from the persona work, also needs to be developed. This process can in itself be a very useful test as to whether implementing a search solution is actually going to provide value to the user.

Concurrent users

With search applications the load on the various servers and the network in terms of indexing, query processing and document presentation can be quite significant. It is therefore valuable to obtain some sense of any search scheduling issues, such as a group of users running standard enquiries at the beginning of the day, or just before going to a monthly meeting. A few search engine vendors also cost out their licences on a maximum number of concurrent users, though this is becoming quite uncommon.

Document security

In general, document security in organizations tends to be managed on an ad hoc basis, often based on a physical security model where documents with specific security classifications are held in designated filing cabinets. There are, of course, many instances, especially in the defence industry, where there is a more rigorous approach to document security, in line with:[6]

- ISO/IEC 17799:2005 Code of practice for Information Security Management
- ISO/IEC 27001:2005 (formerly BS 7799-2:2002) Specification for Information Security Management.

Considerable care will be needed to ensure that an enterprise search implementation does not invalidate a corporate code of practice, and developing an appropriate metadata schema may prove a substantial challenge.

The problem is usually caused by e-mail. The author of the document saves the confidential document to a convenient server, and may give it an innocuous file name. The existence of the document is then notified to a small group of people. Unbeknown to the author, the search engine crawler has already found the new document and indexed it, potentially revealing it to the entire organization.

If the enterprise search is being carried out on a multinational basis the problems are even more acute, because there needs to be a totally consistent approach to document security management across the organization. The English-language version of a document may be securely stored, but a version in another language may have been inadvertently placed on an unsecured server.

IT architecture considerations

The importance of considering the IT architecture of the organization and the potential impact of adding possibly multiple servers must be taken seriously. Users are already used to a speed of response from Google and other web search engines which is impossible to achieve in an enterprise implementation, and so will need to have their expectations managed from the outset.

Even if the query and results presentation are carried out quite quickly, delays in retrieving the documents will result in much user dissatisfaction. Few users will have any idea of the processing that is taking place behind the scenes.

It is probably unlikely that an enterprise search can be implemented on the existing server array, especially if there is going to be a requirement to provide access to large documents (or sections of documents) across the enterprise. Some of these documents may be very large PDF files, PowerPoint files or images, and the implications for bandwidth need to be considered carefully. The scale of the server and bandwidth requirements may be difficult to establish at the outset of the project, and there may well be a requirement for load balancing.

Especial care needs to be taken if a federated search is being considered that might cover enterprise resource planning (ERP) and client management applications This may well place new demands on these applications, and their update plans may need to be reviewed.

One three-letter acronym often used in connection with search software is API, application program interface. An API is a software routine for integrating other applications with the search engine, or writing customized search results screens. All search engine vendors have libraries of these routines that they have developed over the years. The extent to which these APIs can be used directly in a specific application varies considerably, depending on the release version of the search software and the application to which integration is required. Sometimes quite a small change can result in a considerable amount of development work, with existing APIs perhaps needing to be modified as well.

Scalability

It is unlikely that an enterprise search solution will be rolled out across the organization at the outset, especially in multinational organizations. Preparatory work may have to be carried out on a document management system before it is crawled by the search engine, and literally overnight the size and complexity of the search could be significantly increased.

The elements that need to be considered are the following:

- **Indexing** This is very CPU intensive, and although indexing on an incremental basis seems like a good idea in terms of the currency of the document collection, there is an overhead in terms of CPU requirement that needs to be quantified. The fundamental aspect of hash tables is that they are designed to be rebuilt with very little effort, but this will vary from vendor to vendor, and from document collection to document collection.
- **Querying** In general this requires relatively little processing, as all that is being undertaken is a look-up against a set of database tables. However, if it is necessary to check against an access control list to determine whether the searcher can see specific documents, there is more processing to undertake, especially if this is done on the search results.

- **Results presentation** This aspect is a more complex one to address, as it will be affected both by the performance of the server on which the document(s) reside and by the size of the files concerned. Although most corporate networks should have enough capacity to cope with the transmission of large files, there may well be offices in some countries that do not have adequate bandwidth. The requirements of employees accessing search over mobile/wireless links also need to be taken into consideration.
- **Storage** Fortunately, storage capacity is relatively inexpensive, but unlike server performance/bandwidth issues (where the performance may be degraded but will still work) a lack of storage is more fundamental. The rate of increase in storage requirements will need to be worked out in discussion with the vendor. The capacity planning guidelines used for structured databases do not apply.

The need for a team effort

The range of information needed to specify an enterprise search application is very wide indeed, and it is very unlikely that there will be one single person in the organization who has all this information. A team-based approach is essential, based on the following elements:

1. **Document group** - determining the volume, rate of growth and file characteristics of the document collection, and considering metadata/taxonomy issues
2. **Technology group** - assessing the current information systems architecture, future requirements to accommodate an enterprise search application, and the implications for integration with other applications
3. **User requirements group** - understanding the needs of users, and subsequently managing the usability tests.

As an indication of the relative allocation of effort, probably around 60% of the total project effort needs to go into the specification of requirements. This will mean that the process of selecting a vendor is as straightforward as possible, and overall might account for a further 15% of the total effort. That leaves 25% to be allocated to the implementation and initial tuning of the search engine after installation. Needless to say, a task of this complexity needs strong project management, and a committed sponsor.

If the organization does not have a sponsor for the project from the outset, an experienced project manager, and staff with the skills and time to undertake the initial research and analysis work, then the prospects for a successful procurement and implementation will be seriously jeopardized.

Schedule for the selection process

The selection of an enterprise search engine cannot be accomplished in a few weeks, even if the outcome of the analysis is that an out-of-the-box or search appliance solution will be the most effective implementation route. The set of work elements in Table 5.1 is presented as an indicative guide.

It is difficult to give an average duration for this process, but for a web or intranet application it could take perhaps three months, and for an enterprise application nearer a year in total.

Knowing what you don't know

The essential first step in implementing a search engine is to understand what is not known about the issues that will affect the selection and implementation. The CMS business is now quite well documented and understood, but that is not the case with search engines. There needs to be a period of basic research, including quite a detailed review of the different technological approaches that have been developed by the search engine vendors. The variation in approach is much higher than is currently the case for CMS applications.

Every organization will have its own corporate style of setting out an invitation to tender for a software application. The set of headings below are therefore more of a checklist to ensure that all the key information is presented to the vendor, even if the section headings themselves are different.

Although there are fewer search engine vendors than CMS vendors there is much to be gained from developing a list of perhaps a dozen or so possible vendors, rather than sending out the tender documentation to a list two or three times that size.

Table 5.1 Work elements for implementing a search engine

Phase	Comments
Research	Read through briefing papers from vendors Review published articles Talk to organizations who have implemented a search engine Establish a project team Agree the initial schedule
Discovery	Document audit User needs determined through personas Review of IT implications, including integration Initial shortlist of potential vendors Determine in-house skills
Business case	Determine budget Develop business case NB: Discovery and business case work can be undertaken in parallel
Preparation of the RFP	At this stage it may be helpful to send out an Expression of Interest letter to potential vendors
Vendor response	This assumes that there has been some initial contact with the vendor, and the company is aware of the schedule for the procurement
Vendor meetings	Before the presentations themselves it can be valuable to have meetings with the vendors to review the tender documentation and to agree the basis for the presentation. This may not always be possible under the procurement rules of the organization, and much will also depend on the location of the vendor's offices
Presentations	Finding a time when all the members of the project team are available may be difficult
Reference site visits	These may take some time to set up and may involve travel to another country
Pilot test with sample collection of documents	This could be done in parallel with other post-presentation activities
Contract negotiations	Only at this stage will a firm price be established
Initial implementation	This depends on the availability of appropriate hardware and the specialists from the vendor
First round of optimization	

Even at this stage it is important to set up a project team to manage the selection and procurement process. This may well not be the same as the team that manages the implementation, as a different set of skills will be required, including a higher level of involvement from the IT department.

Developing the request for a proposal (RFP)

Every organization has its own three-letter acronym for the document to send out to vendors, and indeed there may well be a standard format for such documents. If there is, then care needs to be taken to ensure that the format reflects appropriately the requirements for search software.

Independent of the format, the information that should be presented in the RFP should include the following:

- **The business objectives** It can be of great assistance to a vendor to understand the business objectives behind the decision to purchase an enterprise search application. Often this analysis can indicate some of the organizational politics behind the decision. It may be that there is an underlying problem with the current search engine, or that the organization has had a scare through not being able to find business-critical documents within the required timescale.
- **Summary of persona/scenario work** The persona and scenario development (see page 50) will provide an indication of the types of searches that need to be undertaken, and the business context for them. This will assist the vendor in developing demonstrations of their application and selecting possible reference clients.
- **Key features requirement** Setting out a list of 40 specific features is not very helpful. Out of the document analysis, the IT platform analysis and the personas may come some features (such as the support for particular file types, or the need to be able to sort standard searches very easily) that would be important selection criteria.
- **Integration with other systems** These systems should be defined in some detail, setting out not only the application, but also the version of the software and any customization that was carried out. If there has been customization then it is important to state whether

it was the software vendor that carried out the work or an in-house development team. This is not to say that the quality of the work would be any the poorer for being carried out internally, though sometimes the documentation may not be as rigorous.

- **IT platform and IT systems management** As has been emphasized already, setting out in detail the current IT platform and systems management architecture is a basic requirement for the vendor to be able to judge any changes that might need to be made to the system, either at the initial implementation or as the application is rolled out to more servers.
- **Implementation issues** Under this heading the roll-out strategy for the application should be set out. This is also the section in which the current skills and expertise of the development team should be documented, as many search applications fail to run to schedule and budget because the customer either cannot free up the time of current members of staff, or experiences difficulties in hiring staff at short notice.
- **Selection procedure** This section should set out the timescale for the selection procedure, and also outline the selection criteria that will be used in the process.
- **Profiles of key staff on the project team** It can be helpful to have a list of the project team members.

Information from the vendor

There is a tendency to ask a substantial number of irrelevant questions. Certainly an appropriate degree of diligent enquiry into the financial background of the company is essential, but at this point in time the emphasis should be on setting out clearly what the search requirements are.

When reviewing the financial performance of the company it is worth looking at the ratio of licence/product sales to professional consulting, as this may give an indication (and it is only an indication) of the multiplier that might need to be applied to the base licence cost quoted in the proposal, to obtain an indication of the total cost of implementation.

However, the majority of search vendors are either private companies or divisions of major IT companies, and so the amount of financial information that will be disclosed is limited, even under a non-disclosure agreement.

Some other issues worth clarifying at this stage are:

- How will customer service and support be provided to the main locations of the organization?
- If appropriate, would this be on a 24/7 basis?
- What technical support is provided?
- What are the procedures for problem reporting and problem resolution?
- What is the approach for software releases, updates and 'bug' fixes?
- Is there a user group?
- How many current customers does the vendor have?
- How many use the current version/configuration of the product?

At some point in the selection process it is valuable to be able to meet some reference clients, but the most that can be achieved through these visits is to gauge the level of support the vendor has offered. Because of the inevitable differences between the document collections of organizations it is much more difficult to compare search performance than would be the case in comparing the usability of the authoring interfaces of a content management application.

Other factors in setting up reference visits are:

- The installed base of higher-priced solutions is still fairly low, so a visit may have to be made to a site in another country.
- The reference sites may have much higher concerns about information security during a demonstration than would be the case with demonstrating a CMS.
- The search output screens will have been customized to the needs of each client.

Open source software

Comparing open source and commercial off-the-shelf products is not straightforward, as all the normal criteria do not apply, especially those relating to the business performance of the vendor. The focus should be on the way in which product deployment, development and upgrading are supported by the development community that has been built up around the software.

Pilot testing

Evaluating the software with a subsection of the document collection is an essential element of the selection process. The establishment of the test collection should be one outcome of the document audit outlined on page 52. The evaluation criteria need to be mutually agreed. System performance metrics cannot easily be tested in this way, but the ability to format the results pages can assessed, as can the format of the search logs.

There are a number of vendors who offer a free download of their software for evaluation purposes, but care needs to be taken to have a formal evaluation process and to understand clearly what the upgrade paths will be. Search appliances can be purchased and installed very quickly indeed. As a result, the time to install a search engine could be reduced to a month or so, but only in situations where the initial requirements analysis has been undertaken and a clear statement of requirements established. It is these processes that take the time and effort, and are essential to ensuring that organizational and user needs are met.

References

1 Mulder, S. and Yaar, Z. (2006) *The User is Always Right*, Indianapolis IN, New Riders Publishing.

2 Pruitt, J. and Aldin, T. (2006) *The Persona Lifecycle: keeping people in mind throughout product design*, San Francisco CA, Morgan Kaufmann.

3 http://research.microsoft.com/research/coet/Grudin/Personas/Pruitt-Grudin.pdf.

4 http://research.microsoft.com/research/coet/Grudin/Personas/Grudin-Pruitt.pdf.

5 www.steptwo.com.au/papers/kmc_personas/.

6 www.bsi-emea.com/InformationSecurity/Overview/index.xalter.

Chapter 6

Optimizing search performance

In this chapter:

- The parameters of search engine performance
- Search engine tuning
- Using web analytics software
- Data privacy issues

Introduction

The previous chapter outlined the elements that go to make up a search application, whether for a website or an enterprise. A major challenge for the organization is then to make sure that the entire system works as effectively as possible. For better or worse, Google has set some standards for search performance, but these are mainly in terms of systems performance and the time taken to run a query against an index of the spidered web. Users of websites in particular, but also users of enterprise search applications, use Google as a benchmark when judging search performance.

Optimizing search performance requires attention to be paid to three different but related areas:

- the performance of the search system
- the usability of the search application
- the extent to which the search provides the information being sought.

Search system performance

Some search vendors display the time taken to undertake a search as a metric of search performance. Obviously system response speed is important, but it is doubtful whether the user actually cares how long it took so long as it took no longer than they expected, even though they would not be able to specify in tenths of a second how long that is. Among the factors that need to be tracked on a regular basis are:

- average response time for different types of query (which requires a definition of query types)
- average time taken to retrieve and then present individual documents or groups of documents from each server
- time taken to update the indexes (measured in megabytes per hour).

The initial indexing can be quite a prolonged exercise. A representative time might be of the order of 10 Gb/hour. Subsequent updates to this will be much quicker.

In an enterprise application the system response times for queries and document presentation are determined by the organization's server/network architecture. This may vary with the time of day, the day of the week and many other factors, because certainly as far as the network is concerned the latency will be affected by other activities taking place over it. The time taken to run the query will be affected by the way the indexing server is optimized. The time to display a given document may well vary considerably, depending on the location of the server and what other transactions are taking place at the same time.

In general, users will accommodate delays in response times of the order of one or two seconds. Any longer than this and there is a concern that the search engine is not working correctly (especially at the query stage), and the level of trust in the search results will therefore be diminished.

One factor that will affect the query performance is the indexing schedule. This is very processor-intensive, and if the index is being totally rebuilt (perhaps on a weekly basis) the timing of this must be carefully determined so that offices in different time zones are not caught out by slow response times. Index throughput also needs to be monitored: it could be that a network connection has degraded or a server configuration has been changed.

In general, web searching is much less processor-dependent and because the files are much smaller there are unlikely to be any problems arising from network bandwidth.

System availability

A number of service levels need to be defined as regards system availability. These are of much greater significance in a large enterprise environment, or for a hosted web search application, but the general principles apply to all search implementations:

- **Availability** This sets the level at which search should be available. For a website for a multinational implementation this needs to be at, or very close to, 24x7x52, but for a small intranet it may be permissible for the system to be offline overnight.
- **Downtime** Although search itself may be available on a 24x7x52 basis it may be necessary to carry out unplanned fixes to the indexing spiders and administration tools. These are usually expressed in terms of hours per month.
- **Planned maintenance** This is different from downtime, in that it sets out the standard maintenance schedules for tasks such as server management and making changes to the administrative applications. The indexes may well need to be defragmented periodically, and there needs to be as much free storage on the index server as the index itself for this to be accomplished. While this is being undertaken no indexing can be carried out, so the defragmentation schedule needs to be planned with care. The more often an index is updated, the more frequent will be the need for defragmenting.
- **Reliability** Included under this heading are the extent to which the

indexing is carried out successfully (how often are document missed) and an acceptable number of problems that can arise. In any month there may be times when one of the servers goes down, but because of load balancing this has little impact. However, if the index becomes corrupted in some way this will have a very serious impact on the level of service.

- **Support** The availability of helpdesk and technical support from the vendor (and, where appropriate, the systems integrator) needs to be clearly established. However, the detail needs to go beyond the 'opening hours' and set out desirable resolution times as well as the procedure to identify and resolve 'red flag' issues that would put the availability and performance of the search application at risk. Agreeing the service levels will be especially difficult where there is more than five hours' time difference between the customer site and the helpdesk location.
- **Backup** All IT applications have a backup schedule, but it is important to have a backup schedule not only for the indexes and taxonomies but also for the administrative files that contain all the search logs and security management applications.
- **Disaster recovery** IT departments will have standard disaster recovery procedures, but with a process as dynamic as search it is important to state what the ideal is in terms of the last stable state of the indexes in particular.
- **Monitoring and reporting** This sets out the standard log files that will be available, and their format, covering metrics such as number of concurrent users, resources used for each search, search terms used, and the number of documents downloaded.

Search engine tuning

The process of optimizing a search application is usually referred to as tuning, and needs to be undertaken on a continuous basis. At the heart of search engine tuning are the search log files, and the ease with which these can be generated and formatted varies considerably between vendors. As the process of tuning is so important, it is equally important to review the types of report that can be generated during the vendor selection process. There are also third-party applications, such as the SearchTracker from New Idea Engineering, a US-based search consultancy, which is a specialized Java proxy server that logs user searches to a relational database to provide fast-response detailed drill-down activity reports.[1] Other web analytics products are listed in Table 6.1.

Table 6.1 Web analytics tools

Click Tracks	www.clicktracks.com/
Coremetrics	www.coremetrics.com
Google Analytics	www.google.com/analytics/
Nedstat	www.nedstat.com
NetInsight	www.unica.com/
Omniture	www.omniture.com/
SAS	www.sas.com/solutions/intellivisor
ViviStat	www.visistat.com/
Visual Sciences	www.visualsciences.com/
WebSideStory	www.websidestory.com
WebTrends	www.webtrends.com/

Some of these are best suited to website analytics, and the extent to which the logs from a search engine can be managed with these products should be verified at the start of the selection process.

There is now considerable interest in web analytics, and two books have recently been published on this topic.[2,3] There are a number of ways in which relevancy can be improved. However, to do any of these without some metrics about how the system and the users react to the changes is very risky. This is where the careful analysis of search logs is invaluable.

One of the easiest to accomplish is to weight the relative weight of a search term depending on which element of the document the word appears in. The main field elements are usually:

- title
- summary

- keywords
- text
- metadata.

Although the title might be seen as the most important element, this may not always be the case. A good example would be in PowerPoint presentations, where the three-year plan for the organization might have been entitled 'Onwards and Upwards'. The words in the Agenda slide would be a much better indication of the content of the presentation. Another useful weighting factor is when all the words in a query appear in the same sentence. However, all these weighting factors need to take account of the content being searched, and should not be applied across all searches and all content.

Top searches

This log report sets out the number of searches performed based on the queries used, and so gives a ranked list of keywords. The search analytics program should contain a decomposer that takes multiple keywords used in a query and transforms them into individual keywords. This log needs to be interpreted with some care, as some search engines may transform the query into something rather different to use as a query against the index files. There is no better option than to work through the log to identify changes that could be made to improve the search results. It can be useful to identify the number of hits that have been presented for the query to see if problems may be arising in terms of too many pages of hits. The search team itself needs to run the searches as well to look at how long the relevancy tail is for the search.

Top content

This is especially useful in reviewing searches of web content. The number of hits on the page from the search box compared with the number of hits from the page navigation may give an indication as to whether the page is perhaps hidden away in the site, and could usefully be promoted, or even made into a quick link.

Bottom searches

The opposite of top is bottom, but this designation is not quite appropriate. At the bottom of the keyword ranking there may be search terms that are misspelt, or possibly acronyms (or the full word sequence) that are not related in a synonym directory.

No-results

These are especially important to consider, as there is nothing more frustrating than not finding any information. The reasons for this type of outcome include there being no information on the site, misspelling of a search term, or (more likely) the content has not been indexed. This can occur because the content is on a server location that has not been spidered, the information is in a scanned PDF and cannot be indexed, or the person undertaking the search does not have authority to read the content the query might return.

Privacy issues

A major issue with search log analysis, especially in the EU, is data privacy. In reviewing intranet search logs there could be searches on voluntary redundancy, sexual harassment or discrimination, or for the addresses of senior staff. All these might be taken as an indication that the person carrying out these searches was planning to take redundancy, sue the organization for sexual harassment or discrimination, or send the addresses of senior managers to an animal rights activist group. The extent to which search logs might be construed to contain personal information has not been tested in the courts, but the issue has come to the top of the agenda of data protection managers and legislators after AOL published details of the search logs of over 650,000 subscribers in July 2006.

Many countries have rigorous data protection legislation, with the member states of the EU being at the forefront in developing such legislation. The legislation is somewhat complex.[4] At the heart of the EU legislation is Directive 95/46/EC of the European Parliament and of the Council of 24 October 1995 on the protection of individuals with regard to the processing of personal data and on the free movement of such data. Each member state of the EU has implemented this Directive within its own legal framework, so that the protection an individual has is consistent across all member states.

Many other countries also have data privacy legislation, but the EU only recognizes that in three EEA member countries (Norway, Liechtenstein and Iceland) as being equivalent. In the case of Switzerland, Canada, Argentina, Guernsey, Isle of Man and the US Department of Commerce's Safe Harbor Privacy Principles, the Commission regards these as providing adequate protection with some caveats.

The USA takes a different approach to privacy from that taken by the EU. The USA uses a sectoral approach that relies on a mix of legislation, regulation and self-regulation. The EU relies on comprehensive legislation which, for example, requires the creation of government data protection agencies, registration of databases with those agencies, and in some instances prior approval before personal data processing may begin. As a result of these different privacy approaches, the Directive initially had some very significant effects on the ability of US companies to engage in transatlantic dealings. To overcome these problems the US Department of Commerce and the European Commission developed a 'Safe Harbor' framework, which was approved in July 2000. In effect, this commits companies using the protocol to manage data privacy to the same levels in the USA as they would have to in the EU.

Participation in the Safe Harbor is entirely voluntary. Organizations that decide to participate must comply with the Safe Harbor's requirements and must publicly declare that they do so. To be assured of Safe Harbor benefits, an organization needs to self-certify annually to the Department of Commerce in writing that it agrees to adhere to the Safe Harbor protocol. It must also state in its published privacy policy statement that it does so.

The implications of this legislation and the Safe Harbor protocol is that only US companies working within the protocol can process personal data in the US from their operations in the EU. There is also a very important distinction between personal information and sensitive personal information. Sensitive personal information covers:

- the racial or ethnic origin of the data subject
- their political opinions

- their religious beliefs, or other beliefs of a similar nature
- whether or not they are a member of a trade union
- their physical or mental health or condition
- their sexual life
- the commission or alleged commission by them of any offence.

One key issue is that a person must give their informed consent for this information to be held in a database. To develop a scenario, assume that the HR database of a US organization in Europe contains, with their permission, information on the racial or ethnic origin of staff. Assume also that someone in the US wanted to check on which members of staff had a particular ethnic origin. The first issue is whether data privacy legislation would allow someone in the US to carry out that search; this might well require authorization under the Safe Harbor protocols, and if such authorization has not been received, the search logs, in revealing the search, could potentially put the search team under a requirement to inform the organization that such a search had been carried out.

It must be understood that this is a hypothetical scenario, and is included only to highlight the complexities of data privacy legislation and the fact that, to date, search logs have probably escaped our attention. The AOL release of search logs has certainly changed that.

References

1. www.ideaeng.com/ds/searchtrack.html.
2. Rosenfeld, L. and Wiggins, R. (2007) *Search Analytics for Your Site: conversations with your customers*, Ann Arbor MI, Rosenfeld Media, www.rosenfeldmedia.com.
3. Inan, H. (2006) *Search Analytics: a guide to analyzing and optimizing website search engines*, Sydney, Australia, www.hurolinan.com/.
4. http://ec.europa.eu/justice_home/fsj/privacy/index_en.htm.

Chapter 7

Search usability

In this chapter:

- The importance of search usability
- Options for presenting search results
- Three case studies of excellence in search usability

Supporting information discovery

Usability is a measure of the ease with which someone can make use of a system to undertake specific tasks. Over the last few years there has been a very significant increase in the level of interest in usability as organizations strive to get the best returns out of their investment in websites.

Among the elements of usability are:[1]

- **Functionally correct** - the system allows the user to undertake the task
- **Efficient to use** - the time and/or number of clicks that are taken to perform the task
- **Easy to learn** - the task requires only a few clicks and advice is provided (or is available) to assist the process
- **Easy to remember** - the system does not tax the human memory

- **Error tolerant** - the user is never left at a dead end and there are routines that track problems as they arise and enable designers to take remedial action
- **Subjectively pleasing** - users want to use the system because of the overall 'feel' of the site and the way in which it reacts to their requirements.

Although there is a vast literature on usability testing there is very little advice on usability issues regarding search. Even the normally invaluable Useit website from Jakob Nielsen[2] has only a few comments on search among the several hundred other entries. Probably the best general resource on the design of search pages is the much-expanded chapter on search in the third edition of Morville and Rosenfeld's *Information Architecture for the World Wide Web*,[3] and Jenifer Tidwell's book on designing interfaces[4] is also a valuable resource.

Search in particular has to be a dialogue, because of the need for the search engine to assist the visitor/user to determine what they already know and then how they wish to proceed with the next stage of the search. The page navigation on a site is more about presenting terms that the visitor/user will be familiar with as a starting point, and then supporting working down through some form of hierarchy to find the information required. This is, of course, a simplistic view of navigation versus search, and elsewhere in this book the point has been made that search and navigation must be complementary.

There are three aspects to designing search to make the process as effective as possible:

- the positioning of the query box and how this is supported
- the presentation of an individual search result
- the options presented on the screen to support the next stage of search.

The query box

By convention this box is usually placed at the top right-hand end of the toolbar, or sometimes at the top left-hand end, but certainly it is placed on every page. In most websites and intranets the box tends almost to be hidden, as though this is a last resort, rather than given any degree of prominence. Perhaps the reason for this is that often the organization knows that the search feature is not effective, and so hides the box away.

Although it is probably unreasonable to have the query box in the middle of the screen, if the organization wants visitors/users to make full use of the search function then it deserves more prominence. In an intranet situation, and certainly in an enterprise search situation, there will need to be some introductory text about the servers that are indexed by the search engine, and guidance as to the best way to conduct the search. There seems to be no good reason for not adding a click in order to open up the query box in a new page or the next page, so that the visitor/user is presented with guidance and options from the outset, rather than assuming that everyone knows how to search and what to search.

One aspect to consider is whether the search term should remain in the query box once the search has taken place. It would seem preferable to continue to display this, rather than blank out the box and just repeat the search term in the results page.

Search hit presentation

The next step is to look at the information provided about each hit. Typically, a search engine will offer some or all of the following options:

- **Author** For intranet use the author of a document, and/or the department, can be a helpful indication of the value of the document, but this element, like the date, may not be easy to capture from the document.
- **Date** The incorporation of a date is fraught with problems of misinterpretation. The ideal would be the date when the document was prepared, but this metadata element may not have been included when the file was added to the repository. The date that the document was either added to the repository, or was indexed, is worse than useless. The date a document was last reviewed can be very useful to confirm that a policy document is in fact the current version, but this requires good content management policies.

- **Categorization** Some sites present the results in a series of categories. Examples include Mondosoft (www.mondosoft.com) and the UK's National Statistics Service (www.statistics.gov.uk). The National Statistics Service sets out results in three categories, Data Results, Product Results and Source Results, but the outcome for the searcher is the need to scroll down the page to decide whether there is any duplication, and it also presupposes that the searcher knows the difference between the categories.
- **Document title** This should be meaningful, and not truncated to fit into a line width. All too often titles are meaningless because of poor content quality management. Such titles must be identified and changed, not only because they inhibit the initial comprehension of the value of the search result, but because one of the most useful relevance functions is to put more weight on words that appear in the document title.
- **File format** This can be a useful way of assessing the value of a document, especially an Excel file or a PowerPoint presentation, as this will indicate the type of content that is likely to be found in the document.
- **File size** If the intention is to download the document, some indication of file size can be useful. Large Excel files can be quite unmanageable and may well be databases masquerading as spreadsheets. Large PowerPoint files can present major download and printing problems. Although the enterprise network may be broadband the user may be accessing the database over a lower-speed network, especially in the case of a website.

  In theory this should not be a problem, because there should be content standards that ensure there is no document on the system larger than (say) 500 Kb, and that if there is then the document is segmented into smaller sections.

  If it is decided to provide a numeric file size, then taking up space telling a searcher that the file size of the document is 15.7 Kb is a waste of space. The rate at which dial-up access is being replaced by broadband services means that indicating file sizes in excess of 100 Kb is probably sufficient.

- **Hyperlink** The hyperlink is more than just a way to access the document. If the hyperlink can be intuitively parsed by the searcher then it may reveal a section of the site that has been overlooked. When the hyperlink is a dynamic page session URL then it has no value at all, and is best omitted.
- **Keyword occurrence** The number of occurrences of a keyword in a document can provide some indication of the document's value, though of course even one occurrence could provide a highly valuable document. In general, the keyword occurrence frequency is best kept within the relevance algorithm, rather than being included in the metadata around a specific result.
- **Keyword in context** The ability to highlight words or phrases within a document that have been used in the search query is not only desirable but almost mandatory. What should be under some degree of user control is the extent of the context provided, for example two lines either side of the words, or the complete paragraph.
- **Relevance** There are a number of ways to present this information, from a number of stars to percentage relevance. All depend on some form of statistical analysis of the frequency and distribution of the keywords in the document, and the extent to which they help in enterprise search is open to serious question. Even for a website, stating the relevance in either percentage terms or as a star rating may not be all that helpful to the searcher.

  The assumption is that the default return will be hits in decreasing order of relevance. What can be quite alarming to the searcher is when the top document has a relevance of significantly less than 100%. There may be good reasons for this, but it can be disconcerting.

  Relevance can be of use to provide some indication of how long the 'tail' of the results set is: has the relevance dipped to 50% by the second page, or are there many pages of highly relevant hits? Another value of relevance is when the results are sorted by date or some other parameter, such as file type.

  The most concise way of presenting relevance is by percentage rather than stars, but perhaps the percentages should be rounded to the nearest 5%, assuming that the search engine can accomplish this.

- **See similar** This option has virtually no value unless it is made very clear to the searcher what 'similar' means. It would not be a document with the same relevance, as this would have been adjacent to the result in any case.
- **Summary** A summary of the document can be created automatically by the search engine. The value of this needs to be considered carefully, and the ability of the search engine to provide a meaningful summary of the documents on a specific site or intranet should be assessed at the outset. It may be useful to differentiate between an author summary and a software-generated summary.

Search page presentation

There are three elements to the presentation of the search page itself:

- the response from the search engine about any issues with the search
- the way in which the list of results can be ordered
- suggestions for other categories of search term.

Search failure

There should never be the single response line 'There are no documents which matched your search. Please use a different search.' The main reason for this is that the query term has not been spelt correctly - but then spelling variants should be included in the search engine dictionary.

Too many hits

The search engine should be configured so that any result set larger than three or four pages of hits should generate a warning to the searcher that this is going to occur, or at least recognize that it has. The options should be to refine the search, accept the totality of the hits, or to display a defined number. All popular terms that might give rise to long results lists should have been identified during the preparation phase, arising out of the content audit.

Results presentation

The way in which the results are presented will have a significant impact on the overall usability of the site.

Hits per page

Linked to the scrolling issue is the number of hits to be displayed per page. For browsing this could be quite high (say 25), whereas for other types of search it might be much lower, but with additional information provided for each hit.

Moving between hits

Is this accomplished by clicking on each one, or by the Enter key displaying the next document in the list?

Moving to another page of hits

Most search engines provide the ability to select pages of hits from a list that goes from 1 to whatever is the final page. Rarely is any searcher arbitrarily going to go to the ninth page of hits just to see what is there when the documents are ranked by relevance. This may not be the case if they are ranked in date order, or some other parameter, as it may be useful to jump to page 6 to see if this is where the results for 2004 begin, though there are other ways of managing this.

Page scrolling

As with any web browser application a decision needs to be made as to whether the results should be presented on a screen-page-by-screen-page basis, or whether scrolling should be permitted. If scrolling is permitted, care needs to be taken that all the essential information (such as the search query statement) can be easily seen. In the case of the RNIB site cited below on page 84, some of the very useful options were only presented at the bottom of the page of each set of search results.

Time taken to undertake the search

This may be a feature of public web search engines (even though it is meaningless), but has no place in an enterprise search other than as an element in the administration files.

Save search profile

This capability allows a user, once they have perfected their searching criteria, to save the query by giving it a name. The purpose of this is to save the time invested in refining a query that the user may desire to run again.

Additional functionality in Save Search would allow the user to convert the passive (run on demand) query into an active one that runs in the background, alerting them to new/revised content found.

Save search results

This feature enables the user to review a set of documents offline, so that individual documents can be read and assessed, and then perhaps used as the basis for a further search. This could be undertaken in two ways:

- specifying the number of documents to be saved
- clicking on the documents that need to be saved.

Re-sorting and ranking of results

This should be able to be carried out on any sequential element of the metadata, for example:

- by type of file (i.e. PowerPoint only)
- by size of file/number of pages
- by number of occurrences of the keyword, or whatever relevance algorithm is being used
- by language
- by class of document
- by author/department.

Ideally, it should be possible to go back sequentially through the re-sorts that have been tried, rather than having to remember which presented the best view of the results. However, the metadata must be available to enable these ranked lists to be generated.

Categories

Many search engines provide a presentation of categories alongside the hits. Attention should also be paid to how this is laid out and used to refine a search. The screen space occupied by the category list will inevitably encroach onto the presentation of hits.

Some examples of good search presentation

There are far too few websites that show search implementation as it should be. This section illustrates three quite different sites which exemplify a considered approach to search functionality.

Examples:

- Royal National Institute of the Blind (RNIB)
  www.rnib.org.uk
  pp 84–5
- USA.gov
  www.usa.gov
  pp 86
- Nature
  www.nature.com
  pp 86–7

Example 1: RNIB

The first of these is the UK Royal National Institute of the Blind (www.rnib.org.uk). The query term used is 'detached retina' (see Figure 7.1).

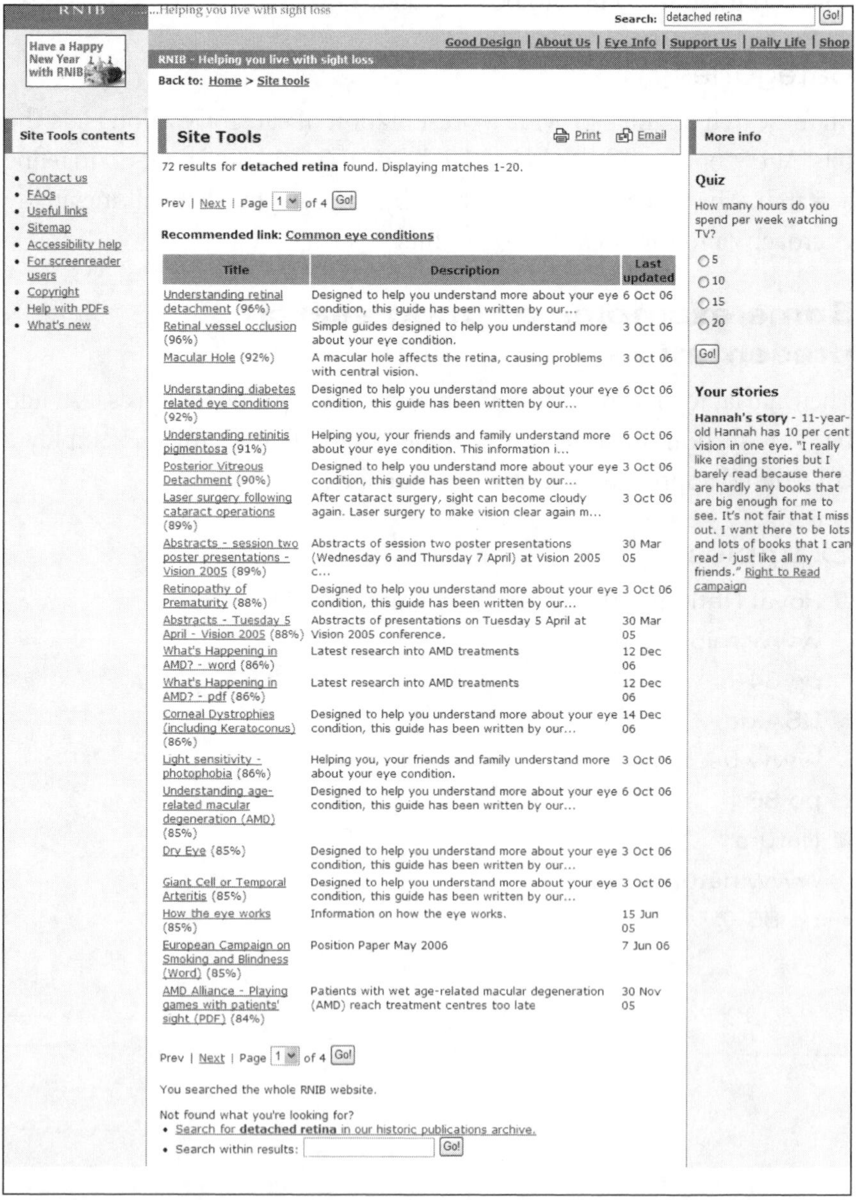

RNIB ...Helping you live with sight loss

Search: detached retina Go!

Have a Happy New Year with RNIB

Good Design | About Us | Eye Info | Support Us | Daily Life | Shop

RNIB - Helping you live with sight loss

Back to: Home > Site tools

Site Tools contents

- Contact us
- FAQs
- Useful links
- Sitemap
- Accessibility help
- For screenreader users
- Copyright
- Help with PDFs
- What's new

Site Tools Print Email

72 results for **detached retina** found. Displaying matches 1-20.

Prev | Next | Page 1 of 4 Go!

Recommended link: Common eye conditions

Title	Description	Last updated
Understanding retinal detachment (96%)	Designed to help you understand more about your eye condition, this guide has been written by our...	6 Oct 06
Retinal vessel occlusion (96%)	Simple guides designed to help you understand more about your eye condition.	3 Oct 06
Macular Hole (92%)	A macular hole affects the retina, causing problems with central vision.	3 Oct 06
Understanding diabetes related eye conditions (92%)	Designed to help you understand more about your eye condition, this guide has been written by our...	6 Oct 06
Understanding retinitis pigmentosa (91%)	Helping you, your friends and family understand more about your eye condition. This information i...	6 Oct 06
Posterior Vitreous Detachment (90%)	Designed to help you understand more about your eye condition, this guide has been written by our...	3 Oct 06
Laser surgery following cataract operations (89%)	After cataract surgery, sight can become cloudy again. Laser surgery to make vision clear again m...	3 Oct 06
Abstracts - session two poster presentations - Vision 2005 (89%)	Abstracts of session two poster presentations (Wednesday 6 and Thursday 7 April) at Vision 2005 c...	30 Mar 05
Retinopathy of Prematurity (88%)	Designed to help you understand more about your eye condition, this guide has been written by our...	3 Oct 06
Abstracts - Tuesday 5 April - Vision 2005 (88%)	Abstracts of presentations on Tuesday 5 April at Vision 2005 conference.	30 Mar 05
What's Happening in AMD? - word (86%)	Latest research into AMD treatments	12 Dec 06
What's Happening in AMD? - pdf (86%)	Latest research into AMD treatments	12 Dec 06
Corneal Dystrophies (including Keratoconus) (86%)	Designed to help you understand more about your eye condition, this guide has been written by our...	14 Dec 06
Light sensitivity - photophobia (86%)	Helping you, your friends and family understand more about your eye condition.	3 Oct 06
Understanding age-related macular degeneration (AMD) (85%)	Designed to help you understand more about your eye condition, this guide has been written by our...	6 Oct 06
Dry Eye (85%)	Designed to help you understand more about your eye condition, this guide has been written by our...	3 Oct 06
Giant Cell or Temporal Arteritis (85%)	Designed to help you understand more about your eye condition, this guide has been written by our...	3 Oct 06
How the eye works (85%)	Information on how the eye works.	15 Jun 05
European Campaign on Smoking and Blindness (Word) (85%)	Position Paper May 2006	7 Jun 06
AMD Alliance - Playing games with patients' sight (PDF) (84%)	Patients with wet age-related macular degeneration (AMD) reach treatment centres too late	30 Nov 05

Prev | Next | Page 1 of 4 Go!

You searched the whole RNIB website.

Not found what you're looking for?

- Search for **detached retina** in our historic publications archive.
- Search within results: Go!

More info

Quiz

How many hours do you spend per week watching TV?

- 5
- 10
- 15
- 20

Go!

Your stories

Hannah's story - 11-year-old Hannah has 10 per cent vision in one eye. "I really like reading stories but I barely read because there are hardly any books that are big enough for me to see. It's not fair that I miss out. I want there to be lots and lots of books that I can read - just like all my friends." Right to Read campaign

Figure 7.1 Search results screen from www.rnib.org.uk

Note in particular that:

- The search term is highlighted at the top of the results list as well as appearing in the search box.
- Twenty results are presented on a page, with the means of moving to the next page of results shown at the top of the list, as well as at the bottom.
- The titles are quite descriptive, and there is a good concise summary.
- It is easy for the eye to scroll down the titles, the relevance (in percentage) and the summary.
- There is a clear date showing when the item was last updated.
- There is a recommended link to a term in the RNIB taxonomy that takes the searcher into the relevant section of the site.
- There are options to print the page, and to e-mail the search session to someone else.
- The title is given a relevance ranking, there is a brief description which is in fact the summary of the page, and there is an indication of when the page was last updated. In addition, there is a suggested master link to 'Common eye conditions'.

At the bottom of the page there is the ability to search in the publications archive of the RNIB or to search within the results that were found for the original search. In addition, the option to move to another page of results is repeated.

Given the limited resources that a charity has available this is an excellent example of a good search interface. Most of the design decisions the RNIB makes on the site are very much influenced by the need to ensure accessibility to all of its users, regardless of their disability or what access technology they use. As such it serves as an admirable model for all organizations.

Example 2: USA.gov

For some innovative thinking on search result presentation on a very large site, the US Government USA.gov site provides a good example at www.usa.gov.

Clustering technology from Vivisimo has been used to provide some subject clusters that could be helpful to the site visitor. Of especial note is the option either to open up a link in a new window or to see a preview of the site in a smaller window without leaving the page. The site also offers good search tips and an advanced search option.

There are also links to the home pages of various US Government departments. This is an example of a well designed search page, and there are not many of them.

Example 3: Nature

The third example comes from the scientific journal *Nature* at www.nature.com. The search term used here is 'nanotechnology' (Figure 7.2).

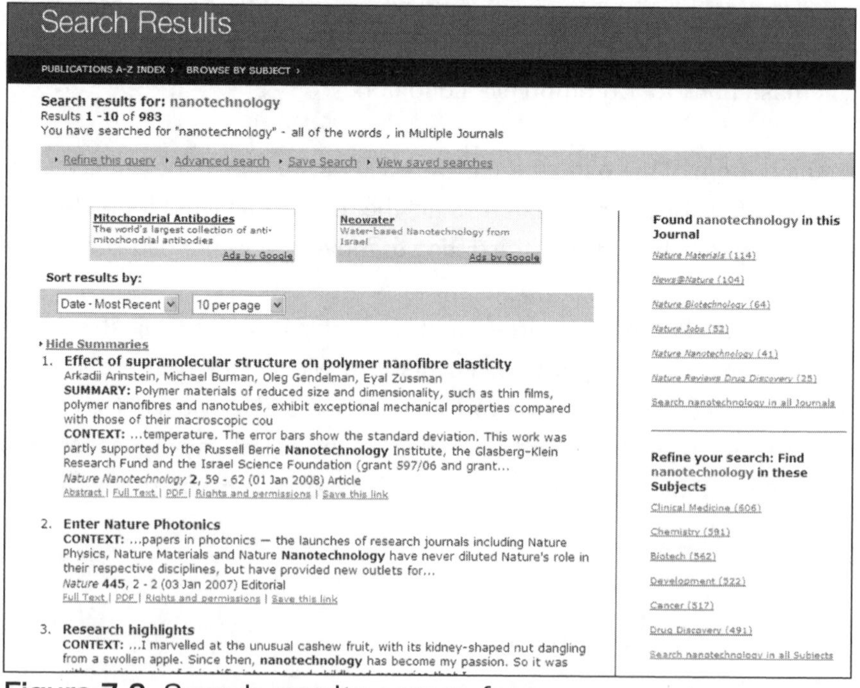

Figure 7.2 Search results screen from www.nature.com – upper section

Note in particular:

- The number of search results per page can be selected from 10, 25, 50 or 100.
- The search results can be saved.
- The results can be sorted by Date – Most Recent, Date – Oldest, Author A–Z, Author Z–A, Title or Journal.
- The search results provide a substantial amount of information, including context and summary in some cases.
- Although specific to a scientific journal, there are options to access the full text of the article as an HTML file, a PDF of the article, and the ability to save the link.
- In the third column options are offered to refine the search through looking just at results for nanotechnology in specific journals published by The Nature Group, looking for results in specific subject areas, and carrying out the search in other search applications.

The site has been optimized for the science community, and the overall impression is a very good one.

A common feature of these examples is the care that has been taken to understand the requirements of users of the website. This is why the use of personas is so valuable in developing a thorough understanding of not only how search will be used, but how it fits within the overall information architecture of websites, intranets and enterprise applications.

Accessibility issues

The issue of legislation to ensure that the needs of disabled employees are accommodated must not be overlooked. There is a wealth of information available on this topic. In the UK the RNIB has been at the forefront in developing accessible websites[5] and there is a similar resource in the USA.[6]

References

1 Gergle, D., Brinck, T. and Wood, S. D. (2000) *Usability for the Web*, New York, Academic Press.

2 www.useit.com.

3 Morville, P. and Rosenfeld, L. (2006) *Information Architecture for the World Wide Web*, 3rd edn, Sebastopol CA, O'Reilly Publishing, www.oreilly.com.

4 Tidwell, J. (2005) *Designing Interfaces*, Sebastopol CA, O'Reilly Publishing, www.oreilly.com.

5 www.rnib.org.uk/xpedio/groups/public/documents/code/public_rnib008789.hcsp.

6 www.usability.gov/accessibility/index.html.

Chapter 8
Desktop search

In this chapter:

- What are the benefits of desktop search?
- What to look for when selecting a desktop search product
- A list of 22 desktop search products

Introduction

The rate of growth in the storage capacity of desktop PCs has been quite extraordinary, with the standard hard drive in a PC being 160 Gb; even in a laptop the standard capacity is 40 Gb. At the same time the number and size of documents being created and stored on a local drive has been increasing at a similar rate – a sort of electronic Parkinson's Law that states that the volume of documents increases to match the memory capacity available. Marshalling all this information into a folder structure is well beyond the capabilities of most of us, as the sheer rate of change in business requires new folders and files to be created without leaving any time to reorganize the existing array. The end result is that it is impossible to find all relevant documents (including e-mails) when responding to a request for information or commencing work on a new document.

Windows XP does have a search feature, but this string-searches files and is a very slow process. For several years there have been indications that Microsoft was planning to launch a more sophisticated search feature in its Longhorn desktop product. This is now called Vista, and by the time this book is published more information should be available on this feature.

Ahead of this a number of the public web search companies launched desktop search software that would build an index of the documents on a hard drive, with Yahoo! and Google being among the early leaders. Over the last two years many other companies have joined the market, and there is now a wide range of products available; these are listed in Table 8.1. These all enable users to index files on their own PCs and laptops, and also on shared public drives.

The role of desktop search

Desktop search is a personal information management application and should not be seen as a low-cost (or even free) alternative to a server-based software application. However, the boundaries will become increasingly blurred as vendors facilitate the indexing of remote and shared drives, and indeed several, such as Isys-Search, Exalead and Google, see desktop search as a way of piloting the functionality of their enterprise search applications.

It is therefore important that selecting a desktop search product is seen as a decision taken in the context of a well developed search strategy for the organization. It is certainly important to take an organization-level view on which desktop product is the most suitable for the way in which employees work, and not to allow individual staff to select whatever product they like. Even desktop search needs to be supported by someone with a good knowledge of PC operating and file management systems, and supporting multiple products is rarely a good approach to effective IT resource management.

One of the benefits of desktop search is that the products do demonstrate many of the features of server-based products, and so provide a means of educating senior managers about the potential benefits of good search functionality.

Selecting a desktop search product

There are a number of features to be considered when deciding on a shortlist of desktop search products.[1,2] In the end, the decision should be made after running the shortlisted products in comparative trials, rather than based on product literature. Among these features are the following:

- **File formats** The list quoted by vendors is often so long that some important omissions may not be spotted. Among the problem formats can be Microsoft PowerPoint, Microsoft Project, Microsoft Visio, Lotus Notes, and databases applications such as Act! Zip files can also cause problems. Over time all the vendors will catch up, and increasingly there will be fewer omissions from the supported file list, but careful checking is essential. Adobe PDF files can be a problem, especially if they are scanned images.
- **Indexing schedule** Indexing is processor-intensive and it is useful to be able to decide when it takes place. Some products index as new content is saved, and others do so on a timed basis. It is very useful to be able to pause or stop the indexing process in the way that most antivirus products work, and this needs to be able to be implemented from soft key designations if at all possible. If indexing is being carried out concurrently with other activities on the PC, then inevitably there will be a reduction in performance. Another feature that can be useful is to be able to specify when applications or folders are indexed, so that e-mails and perhaps a highly used document folder can be indexed more often than a PowerPoint file.
- **Indexing time** The initial process of indexing can take an hour or so, depending on drive capacity and processor speed. During this time any search will result in spurious results, but there should be no excuse for rushing the process. There is a case to be made for rebuilding the index on an occasional basis if there have been major additions or deletions from the hard drives, rather in the way that defragmenting a hard disk can improve performance. It should be possible to undertake this rebuilding without uninstalling and then reinstalling the search software.
- **Index size** Although PCs now have considerable amounts of spare

storage capacity it is important to appreciate that the indexes will themselves need storage space.

- **Folder management** There may be substantial archive files that do not need to be indexed, or perhaps personal files that a user does not wish others to see. It should be remembered that in most organizations anyone can use someone else's PC, and even though they may need to log in, the search products are not linked to the log-in but assume that anyone using the PC has the right to use the search product.
- **Deleted files and folders** One important element of the search management process is the extent to which the product will index deleted files and folders, and whether is there is an option to remove any results from files that were active but were deleted after being indexed.
- **Caching** Google creates a cache that is a text copy of all the documents on the specified drives, and then creates an index from this cache. Although this is claimed to give Google a speed advantage, there is currently the issue that even if a file is deleted a copy will remain in the cache until the drive is reindexed. This could result in deleted documents being listed as hits.
- **External drives** This is a feature that needs special attention as users tend to use a range of external drives, including both magnetic and optical drives, and flash drives. A user may have used a flash drive to transfer a file.
- **Indexing of e-mails** E-mails are probably the most rapidly changing document type on a PC. Although all desktop search products work well with Microsoft Office, there may be some problems with other e-mail clients.
- **Uninstall** When the software is uninstalled the index remains on the hard drive.
- **Product listing** The list of available products is increasing rapidly (see Table 8.1). Many are offered by small software companies, and inevitably the issue of long-term support for their products needs to be factored-in to the implementation decision. The cost of the products ranges from nothing to around $250, with additional charges for

Table 8.1 Desktop search software

Company	Product	URL
Aduna	Aduna Autofocus	http://aduna-software.com
Ask	Ask Desktop Search	www.ask.com
Blinkx	Pico Search and Blinkx Desktop Search	www.blinkx.com/download.html
Copernic	Desktop Search 1.7	www.copernic.com
DiskMETA	diskMeta Personal	http://diskmeta.com
dtSearch	Desktop Search	www.dtSearch.com
EasyReach Corporation	Easyreach Find	www.easyreach.com/
Exalead	Exalead one:desktop	www.exalead.com
Fast Search	Fast PSP (Personal Search Program)	www.fastsearch.com
G10 Software AG	Svizzer Client Personal	www.svisser.com
Google	Google Desktop 4.0	http://desktop.google.com/
iSleuthHound Technologies	The SleuthHound	www.isleuthhound.com/
Isys Software	Isys:desktop 8	www.isys-search.com/products/desktop/index.html
Likasoft	Archivarius 3000	www.likasoft.com/document-search/
Microsoft	Windows Desktop Search	http://desktop.msn.com/
Prodiance	Prodiance Search	www.prodiance.com/products/search.html
Raizlabs Corporation	Magic File	http://raizlabs.com
SearchInform	Searchinform Desktop	http://searchinform.com
Vandenoever	Strigi (open source)	www.vandenoever.info/software/strigi/
Voltix	Voltix Desktop Search	www.voltix.com
X1	Desktop Search	www.x1.com
Yahoo!	Yahoo Desktop Search	http://desktop.yahoo.com/

enterprise-wide licences. There is now an open source desktop search product, Strigi, and this may encourage more developers to enter the market.

References

1 Deegan., P. (2006) *The Desktop Search Handbook*, http://shop.office-watch.com/dsh/.

2 www.goebelgroup.com/desktopmatrix.htm.

Chapter 9

Implementing web search

In this chapter:

- A ten-step procedure that will ensure effective web search implementation

Introduction

Although good web design will assist site visitors to find the information they want through navigation aids and hyperlinks, visitors also expect to be able to search the site. The extent to which there is value in implementing search does depend on the content of the site and the way in which visitors will wish to locate information on it. Adding a search function because of concerns that visitors are not able to use the navigation, and hyperlinking to locate content without an overall consideration of the information architecture of the site, is not the optimal approach. It could well be that search enables the navigation itself to be revised and optimized, removing layers of hierarchy, because search is clearly positioned as a way to find information in document libraries that may well improve the usability of the site to other users.

Search is especially important in e-commerce sites, where there is product- or service-related information. One of the issues in such sites is not just the ability of the search feature to locate products, but also to be able to provide a range of ranking opportunities, such as price, size, colour, and other attributes. Any failure in metadata tagging could result in the product being found in the initial search but not when a ranked list is requested.

As a result faceted search is especially useful in e-commerce applications, and one of the best examples is that of the wine retailer www.wine.com. The Librarian's Internet Index (www.lii.org/), The Gateway (www.thegateway.org/) and the Oracle Press Navigator site (http://pressroom.oracle.com/) are all examples of the Siderean's Seamark Navigator product. There are also a number of search vendors that specialize in e-commerce applications, and these are listed in the Appendix.

The ten-step process to implementing web search

The ten steps are:

Step 1	What will be the benefits to site visitors?
Step 2	Consider the technical options
Step 3	Develop and obtain approval for a business case
Step 4	Write a project plan
Step 5	Agree the outline search parameters
Step 6	Design review
Step 7	Revise the content
Step 8	Select a vendor
Step 9	Install and test for usability
Step 10	Review and revise.

Step 1 What will be the benefits to visitors to the site?

Even if an open source search solution is being considered this is the first question to answer, because if adding search (or a better search) does not result in a better user experience then the resources involved will have been wasted, and could probably have been better spent on enhancing other aspects of the site. Search should not be a belated fix to try to re-energize a site that is not performing as well as expected.

The review process should start with the web statistics. This is an essential requirement. If there are currently no statistics on how the site is being used, then adding in a web statistics package is an immediate priority. The information obtained will not only assist in developing the search features, but will also, in due course, provide essential information on how effective the search implementation has been.[1]

The statistics then need to be matched against a set of personas for the site, so that a view can be taken of which of the personas are likely to make use of search and for what purpose. As with all search implementations, it is important to realize that one size of search does not fit all visitors.

Included in this review should be a consideration of the content of the site, because it could be that the addition of search might enable the content to be enhanced. If the site currently has no search feature, then it might be of benefit to install an open source solution for development purposes that could be used to assess the number of hits on some of the more important keywords. If the site already has a search engine then of course the search logs need to be included in the analysis.

The quality of the content also needs to be assessed. There is nothing more frustrating to a visitor than to see an entry in a list of hits that provides no information about what the hit refers to, such as a hit that just says 'Issue One 2005'.

Step 2 Consider the technical options

There are four technical options available:

- Use an open source software solution.
- Use a hosted search service.
- Use a search appliance.
- Use a commercial search software application.
- Use the search engine that is embedded in the content management software.

Cost should not be the primary selection criterion. The zero initial cost of an open source search solution needs to be set against the development effort that may be required to install and implement it. Even though these products are supported by a large development community, the response to enquiries at a technical or design level may not be immediate. Much will depend on the technical expertise of the web team and/or that of the IT team supporting the website. There may be current expertise in managing an open source product, but is this resident in just one member of staff, exposing the organization to a substantial risk should that person leave?

A hosted service certainly gets over the expertise issue, as the companies offering this service will provide all the technical support required. Hosted search is currently more popular in the USA than in Europe, but this is likely to change over the next few years. The only issues about using an offshore hosting solution are:

- the availability of support during the working day
- legal issues arising from having a contract with a supplier in another country
- any data protection issues arising from having information stored on a server in another country
- cost variations arising from currency fluctuations.

Although a search appliance is sold on a plug-and-play basis the expertise required to install and manage the appliance should not be underestimated. It would certainly be advisable to find another organization that uses such an appliance to obtain a first-hand appreciation of the benefits and issues. In the case of Google there is a good discussion forum with a number of active participants.

Some content management software products (for example ActiveEdition and Stellent) do enable their embedded editorial search functionality to be used as the site search, provided all the content to be searched is in the CMS repository.

At this stage no firm decision should be taken about a preferred solution as there is still work to be done, but some indicative prices should have been obtained and any limitations on the way in which search could be implemented identified.

Step 3 Develop and gain approval for a business case

By this stage the resources needed to implement search will start to emerge; most of these will be in the redesign of the site and the ongoing management of the search feature to ensure optimum performance. Even in a small site the effort involved in supporting search should not be underestimated, and there may well be a justification for adding extra staff to the team. The element most often underestimated is the work involved in enhancing the content on the site, in terms of adding metadata, ensuring that the metadata are consistent, making sure that all HTML files have meaningful titles, and that redundant content is removed. Search is like a magnifying glass and will quickly reveal inadequacies in content scope and quality, and cause visitors to question the organization's commitment to the site.

Hosted search services often quote prices based on parameters such as the number of documents, file size and number of searches, so a view needs to be taken on these early in the development of the business case. The most difficult parameter is the number of searches.

Step 4 Write a project plan

Adding in search is not 'business as usual'. The timing of the selection, installation and implementation of the chosen solution needs to be carefully considered. Even adding a search appliance may create issues over rack spacing in the computer room. Using a hosted service will almost certainly give rise to the need for a review of the contract, because it will be written in terms of the country of origin of the search host. This may take longer than might be anticipated, especially if the organization has no precedent for supply contracts placed in another country.

Ideally the beta version of the new site should be testable on a development server at the host search service.

Step 5 Agree the outline search parameters

This is the point at which the project team needs to develop in some detail the options that are going to be offered to the user. Typically, these would include:

- a choice between a basic search and an advanced search
- the size of the text box
- the information that will be provided on each hit
- the way in which any of this information will be highlighted
- the number of hits that will be displayed on the screen (10 is a base point)
- the logic behind the initial display (relevance, chronology)
- how relevance rankings will be presented, if at all
- the options that will be presented should the number of hits exceed (say) 20
- the options for ranking the hits (relevance, alphabetical, chronological, reverse chronological)
- the options for refining the search, such as searching within results
- the information that will be given to the user about the progress of the search.

These issues are covered in more detail in Chapter 7, but are included here to show where in the process they should initially be considered.

There is a constant debate about the merits of offering basic or advanced searches. The advanced option usually provides the user with a range of choices to search by specified parameters, such as date, or section of the site. Often the jump between the two options is too great. The user is presented with a range of advanced options but may not yet know which of the parameters are going to help in narrowing down the search to a useful number of hits, and may also assume a knowledge of the site which is unwarranted. If the user knew more about which areas of the site held content they were looking for, then they would probably use the page navigation rather than searching the entire site.

One of the problems seems to be in the choice of adjectives. The term 'basic' may create the impression of something that is weak in functionality and performance. Perhaps 'standard search' might create a better impression. The term 'advanced' might be seen to be a reflection of the skills of the searcher and not the range of options offered. In this case 'enhanced' might be a better choice of description.

Step 6 Design review

In this step some mock-ups of the way in which search will be incorporated into the site should be developed. Traditionally the search box has been placed at the right-hand corner of the top navigation bar, but all too often this can result in a very small box that is almost invisible to users. It can be very stimulating to look at a range of websites and construct a table of the approaches used for the search box, especially the icon or word used to initiate the search. Google is proud that the company has brought the search box into the centre of the screen, with good reason.

The review should go further than this because the overall information architecture of the site needs to be considered in the light of the addition of search, or even the addition of a better search engine.

Step 7 Revise the content

At this stage it may well become apparent that work will need to be done on the content itself. Enhancing the headings of the content is essential. A search on the UK government site for 'recycling incentives' produced the following in the initial list of hits:

> Microsoft Word J452 Cov and QA.doc
> Page 89 Risk & Policy Analysts Page 73 Neither issue is likely to be solved by altering the tax itself. However, a tax could be packaged alongside revenue recycling or incentive schemes to improve pesticide practices so as to address the full range of pesticide risk issues. There are two scenarios in this respect: 1) If it were decided that the issues that are covered by a tax will be targeted

Hit results like this are very unhelpful and begin to destroy the trust the user would like to have in the search process. The amount of work that might be involved in identifying poor-quality file naming could be considerable, even with a content management system, and this work needs to be factored into the project plan.

Another aspect of enhancing the content is to ensure that metadata have been correctly and uniformly applied to the content items. If the site has moved from a flat file site to one managed by a CMS, the migration of the pages might have been poorly managed in respect of the addition of metadata to the content. As a result important older content may not be identified as relevant just because of poor metadata. This is where good titles are important, as one of the key elements in the relevance algorithm used by the search engine may be the occurrence of the search term in the title of the content.

Step 8 Select a vendor

The process for selecting a vendor is set out in detail in Chapter 5. The two key points here are that the process should not be rushed, and that it is important to have a file of content that can be used to evaluate the various options under consideration.

Step 9 Install and test for usability

It is very important that time is allowed for adequate usability testing to be carried out. The testing should be based around the tasks that emerge from the persona development process in Step 1. Almost certainly there will be room for improvements. The usability tests should not just focus on the search functionality itself, but also on the overall usability of the site, as search should be an integral part of the overall information architecture and not seen as a point of last resort.

Step 10 Review and revise

The search logs of the site should be reviewed on a regular basis. Statistics on the number of searches alone may not be very helpful, and search statistics always need to be seen within the business objectives and content use of the site, and the paths that are being taken by site visitors. The ongoing review of the search logs and on other web analytic measures needs to be given an appropriate level of priority and resources. The information from the search logs may indicate that visitors are being confused by the information architecture of the site, and are using search as a last resort. If this is the case, there needs to be the commitment and resources to address the information architecture of the site.

Reference

1 Rosenfeld, L. and Wiggins, R. (2007) *Search Analytics for Your Site: conversations with your customers*, Ann Arbor MI, Rosenfeld Media, www.rosenfeldmedia.com.

Chapter 10

Implementing search for an intranet

In this chapter:

- A ten-step procedure that will ensure effective intranet search implementation

The ten-step process to implementing intranet search

Although the basic principles for selecting an intranet search engine are the same as for a web search engine, there are some important differences and hence the steps are somewhat different:

Step 1 What will be the benefits to employees?
Step 2 Consider the technical options
Step 3 Develop and obtain approval for a business case
Step 4 Write a project plan
Step 5 Define a test document set
Step 6 Scope the user interface
Step 7 Select a vendor
Step 8 Install and test for usability

Step 9 Optimize search performance
Step 10 Have a development strategy.

Step 1 What will be the benefits to employees?

Arguably the expectations of employees are much higher than those of a visitor to a website. There is often an alternative website, but in most organizations that have an intranet this is the default information platform, and contains (at least in theory) all the core information an employee needs to meet organizational and personal objectives. The primary role of an intranet is to enable better decisions to be made. Certainly there is a subsidiary role in being a communications channel, but the business case for investing resources in an intranet is increasingly about supporting tasks. Whereas with a website hyperlinks are an important way of supporting information discovery, the scale of an intranet, the diversity of the content and the number of contributors means that hyperlinks are not as rigorously implemented and managed as they are in good websites. There should be no excuse for poorly implemented search in an intranet, as the search function has to make up for the inevitable weaknesses in hyperlinks.

Compared to website statistics, similar information for an intranet, even when it is available, is much less helpful, though of course if the site already has a search engine then the search logs should be carefully reviewed.

In the case of an intranet, its future development within the overall information management strategy of the organization must be considered from the outset. This is because it is likely that other information management applications, ranging from a document management application to an enterprise resource planning application, may end up being accessed through the intranet. As a result, the search functionality on the intranet may need to be extended to provide an enterprise search capability able to search multiple servers and provide both structured and unstructured information.

This would have a very significant impact on the decision concerning the level of investment that would be appropriate to searching just intranet content. There is little point in selecting a low-cost search product that meets the immediate requirements only to have to replace this with an enterprise-level product in the not-too-distant future.

Step 2 Consider the technical options

Although hosted search services are an option for a website, very few organizations are going to feel comfortable using a hosted service for an intranet, and so there are four options:

- Use an open source software solution.
- Use a search appliance.
- Use a commercial search software application.
- Use the search engine that is embedded in the content management software.

One of the considerations in intranet search management is that many intranets are run on Microsoft SharePoint. The search functionality of SharePoint 2003 is weak, especially in the case of the SharePoint Web Services version. Although Windows SharePoint Services 2.0 and Microsoft Office SharePoint Portal Server 2003 used common Microsoft Search technology, users found the two environments to be quite different from one another. In addition, administrators needed to use different tools to configure and manage each environment. As a result, a number of vendors have developed search products optimized to work with Microsoft SharePoint 2003, and these include:

- BA-Insight
- Coveo
- Interse.

In 2006 Microsoft released a substantially revised version of SharePoint Server. Office SharePoint Server 2007 and Windows SharePoint Services will use a common implementation of Microsoft Search, and both users and administrators use a common set of tools to configure and use Microsoft Search.[1] The range of functionality is much greater, and clearly Microsoft regards SharePoint 2007 as an enterprise search platform. Even so, it is likely that the vendors who have offered enhanced search for SharePoint in the past will also redevelop their product range for the 2007 release.

Probably the major issue with the choice of search technology for an intranet is the extent to which the organization may wish to move gradually towards an enterprise search solution in the future.

The options are:

1. Purchase an intranet search solution which does have the potential to provide enterprise search.
2. Purchase a solution which will manage the intranet well, and then replace it in due course with an enterprise solution.
3. Introduce an enterprise solution in due course, but continue to use the intranet solution through federated search.

There are a number of issues to take into consideration (see Table 10.1).

Table 10.1 Options for intranet search extension to enterprise search

	Benefits	Considerations
Purchase an intranet search solution that does have the potential to provide enterprise search	Maintains the vendor relationship Search team gains an understanding of the underlying technology and relevance tuning Maintains the search experience for the user	How scalable is the platform as indexing volumes and use increase? Limits the range of products that can be considered How well specified are enterprise search requirements?
Purchase a solution which will manage the intranet well, and then replace it in due course with an enterprise solution	Cost of implementation is kept to a minimum Speed of implementation is higher, though this is not a concern in the longer term	The change in the user experience could be significant Vendor relationships may be jeopardized The experience gained with the intranet solution may be wasted
Introduce an enterprise solution in due course, but continue to use the intranet solution through federated search	Maintains the user experience, especially regarding relevance ranking	Considerable questions over the effectiveness of federated searching Making the search experience can be complex and time-consuming

Another issue in the selection of intranet search solutions is the extent to which any desktop search product is chosen to test the solutions from vendors such as Isys-Search, Exalead and Fast Search, which see the desktop as very much a component of the intranet solution. This can get complicated. The desktop search solution may already be searching file servers that are being searched by the intranet, and yet the intranet search product will not be indexing the content on PCs and laptops. This could potentially be a confusing situation.

Step 3 Develop and obtain approval for a business case

This will almost certainly be a more extensive document than is the case for a web search implementation. Whereas a website search can be treated as a standalone implementation, the need to interface with perhaps multiple intranets on a global basis, and support the teams that will be involved, needs careful planning and the support of a senior sponsor.

As has been set out in Chapter 4, the business case for intranet search will best be made on a combination of elements, and not just on an ROI basis.

Step 4 Write a project plan

For the same reasons as for the business case, there needs to be a detailed project plan. An important element of this has to be the time needed to ensure that the content is thoroughly reviewed before the search engine is implemented. Usually intranet operations are under-resourced, and senior managers may not fully appreciate the work that has to be carried out before the search software is installed.

Search vendors generally promote their products as being quick to implement, but there is a difference between installation and implementation. Certainly the software can be downloaded, or the appliance installed, in a matter of an hour or so, but without careful preparatory work all that the search function will show is the lack of content quality and consistency.

Step 5 Define a test document set

There is no alternative to testing any search engine, but in the case of intranet search many of the vendors encourage prospective customers to download and test the software prior to purchase. This can be invaluable in gaining a hands-on view of the software, but it is very important that any 'missing' functionality is clearly identified, and the extent to which the evaluation is, or is not, representative of the full product needs to be ascertained very clearly indeed.

This is where much of the preparatory work needs to be focused, and it can be quite time-consuming for even a small organization. Documents may have been placed on a wide range of servers, and although the IT department will know of the existence of the server the department is highly unlikely to know what content is stored on it.

This step is also where the existence or lack of document security procedures becomes obvious, and these need to be put in place and documents classified retrospectively before the search is implemented.

Step 6 Scope the user interface

Based on the results of the persona testing and usability research, much work needs to be done to define the user interface. The options for display are discussed in some detail in Chapter 7, and James Robertson has written the definitive report on this topic.[2]

Step 7 Select a vendor

The process for selecting a vendor is set out in detail in Chapter 5. The two key points to make here are that the process should not be rushed, and the importance of having a test file to evaluate the various options under consideration.

Step 8 Install and test for usability

It is very important that time is allowed for adequate usability testing to be carried out. The testing should be based on the tasks that emerge from the persona development process in Step 1. Almost certainly there will be room for improvement.

The usability tests should focus not just on the search functionality itself, but also on the overall usability of the site, as search should be an integral part of the overall information architecture and not seen as a point of last resort.

Step 9 Optimize search performance

The search logs of the site should be reviewed on a regular basis. Even in a small organization, if the search has been implemented well there will be a considerable number of searches being made each day. Especially at the launch of the intranet, any issues that arise regarding failed searches, or searches that do not return the expected results, will need to be reviewed in some detail.

It can be reassuring to users to know how this process is going to take place. As well as the search logs themselves, there should be an opportunity for employees to meet with the search team so that there is face-to-face feedback about issues that might not be revealed in the search logs. This is especially the case where the logs do not show which documents have been accessed. The search itself may have resulted in quite a number of documents being returned, but none that meet the requirements of the employee.

Step 10 Have a development strategy

As mentioned above, intranet search is often the precursor to enterprise search. Even if this has not been considered in the business plan and the implementation has gone ahead with a product (such as the Google Mini) that is not designed for enterprise-level search, if the intranet search implementation is effective there will soon be a call for the search functionality to be extended to other servers and applications.

References

1 http://office.microsoft.com/en-us/sharepointsearch/FX101729721033.aspx.

2 Robertson, J. (2006) *Improving Intranet Search*, www.steptwo.com.au/products/search/index.html.

Chapter 11
Enterprise search

In this chapter:

- An introduction to enterprise search
- Technology and implementation issues
- A ten-step procedure that will ensure effective enterprise search implementation

Introduction

The term 'enterprise' tends to be widely used in the IT industry to signify a high-performance software application for use by Fortune 500-type companies. Over the last few years there has been much discussion about what the difference is between a web content management application and an enterprise content management (ECM) application. The same applies to the search business, although, in common with ECM applications, there is the sense that these solutions are designed primarily to work behind the corporate firewall.

The concept of enterprise search is to be able to locate information from any specified server/application, which may include not only internal servers but also external information services. This information might be held in:

- unstructured text files (e.g. web and intranet sites, record and document management systems, e-mail servers)
- structured relational databases (e.g. finance systems, enterprise resource planning, customer relationship management)
- video and image collections (e.g. digital asset management, video conference recordings, video training)
- specialized collections (e.g. project management applications, engineering and architectural drawings, maps, geospatial data, genomic databases).

This list is very incomplete, and of course the complexity is increased quite substantially by the extent of language diversity. In many enterprise-level applications the two languages are UK English and American English, and although there are no issues of transliteration and translation, the problems of synonym management (e.g. gas rather than petrol) are very substantial. It does not help that few organizations would have an accurate list of all the database applications and servers that might contain information broadly relevant to the totality of the enterprise.

Another issue with the term 'enterprise' is that it has a connotation of a for-profit organization. The reality is that all organizations are an enterprise when it comes to specifying a search solution.

In many organizations the requirement for enterprise search starts with the need to provide an effective search solution for an intranet. It is often when implementing an intranet search solution that the organization realizes that employees would benefit from access to a wider range of information applications, and then finds that the intranet solution is not adequately scalable in power or extensible in functionality to provide an enterprise search solution. Enterprise search is very challenging for any organization, even with the best available technology, and simply implementing an enterprise search application will almost certainly not meet the expectations of the employees.

Document diversity

In the case of an intranet it is likely that the majority of documents will be either in HTML or in a current version of Microsoft Office or Adobe

Acrobat. Enterprise document collections may well date back many years and be in a wide range of formats. Almost certainly there will be very limited metadata associated with these documents unless they have been created through a document management system, and even in the best-run companies there are likely to be several document naming and numbering schemes. Some documents may only be available as scanned images and not in an ASCII format, adding to the complexity of the situation.

Probably the greatest challenge is determining the security status of a document. At one point in time the circulation may have been substantially restricted for commercial reasons, but now the document may be less sensitive and indeed could be a source of important information. The scale of the work involved in determining security status should never be underestimated, as the people best placed to comment on this may either have left the organization or may now be in a sufficiently senior position that spending time going through documents may be difficult to justify against other operational demands.

When documents are prepared for publication on an intranet attention is usually paid to presenting them in sections, so that download and printing times are reduced, and indeed the document could even be browsed on the screen. This will not be the case with many of the documents prepared for operational purposes within an organization, where the intention was for them to be circulated and read in a paper format.

Structured database integration

Much of the content of value to an organization is stored in structured databases, such as customer relationship management systems and enterprise resource planning (ERP) systems. Often these will have their own search functionality, which will have been optimized for a particular database structure and use. One of the features of a search across a structured database is that the concept of relevance is irrelevant. Either there are data to support a specific query (hence Structured Query Language, SQL) or there are not. A search for customers who have purchased between £1m and £3m of products in the last 12 months will generate a list of all the customers that meet those criteria.

Information technology requirements

The importance of considering the IT architecture of the organization and the potential impact of the addition of possibly several servers must be taken seriously. Users are already used to a speed of response from Google and other web search engines which is impossible to achieve in an enterprise implementation, and so will need to have their expectations managed from the outset. Even if the query and results presentation are carried out quite quickly, delays in retrieving the documents will result in a lot of dissatisfaction. Few users will have any idea of the processing that is taking place behind the scenes.

It is probably unlikely that an enterprise search can be implemented on the existing server array, especially if there is going to be a requirement to provide access to large documents (or sections of documents) across the enterprise. Some of these documents may be very large PDF files, engineering drawings or images, and the implications for bandwidth must be carefully considered. The scale of server and bandwidth requirements may be difficult to establish at the outset, and there may well be a need for load balancing.

Special care needs to be taken if a federated search is being considered that might search across enterprise resource planning (ERP) and customer relationship management applications. This may well place new demands on these applications, and the update plans of these applications may need to be reviewed.

Managing the implementation

Enterprise-level search engines are complex software applications and cannot be downloaded over the internet and installed the same day. They are usually a collection of modules that need to be specified and installed with care, but the work does not stop with the installation. There will be a staged process of implementation across servers and applications, and this could take many months of effort. While this is being undertaken, the way in which the search engine works from a user perspective will almost certainly change with each step of the process, and so a search carried out today may result in a significantly different result or screen display from a similar search carried out a month earlier.

As a result, the implementation process needs to be widely communicated to all employees. However, communication channels are usually managed on a national basis, so every effort needs to be made to determine which is the most effective channel for a more specific channel, subsidiary or division.

Most other IT implementations will be either for a specific function (such as finance) or for a specific country. There may well be multiple CMS or document management products in use within the company, but there is unlikely to have been any similar enterprise-level implementation other than an ERP system, and even that will probably not be used by all employees. This means that there is little or no relevant experience within the organization, and certainly there will be no previous experience of implementing an enterprise search application.

Another factor in the implementation is the availability of staff from the software vendor, as many are quite small companies headquartered in the USA with mainly sales and customer support offices in Europe. Many vendors work through systems implementors and other partners. A multinational implementation may well require working with different companies at each of the locations of the business.

Managing the search team

As mentioned in Chapter 6, tuning the search engine to optimize the user experience is a continual process. This is difficult enough to achieve in an organization which is largely national in location, but providing this support on a pan-national basis is much more difficult. When a search needs to be undertaken the need is almost always immediate, and so there must be helpdesk support on a 24/7 basis, especially if there is laptop access to the network.

A decision has to be taken as to where in the organization the search support team should report. In many organizations content management applications are the responsibility of marketing (for websites) and/or internal communications (for intranets). Although the underlying technology of CMS applications is quite sophisticated, once implemented the CMS can be maintained at a technical level by perhaps one web developer. The demands on information services support are usually limited to ensuring that the servers are available at an acceptable level of up-time and that users can be properly identified at log-in, as so many elements of a CMS depend on permission being granted to undertake specific tasks.

With a search engine the requirements are rather different. There are some substantial technical issues that need to be addressed on a day-to-day basis, and there is also a need to continue to enhance the search process. There is a good case to be made for this team to be managed by the IT department.

Managing the search desktop

Once a search is carried out on multiple applications the question of how best to present the results becomes difficult to resolve. Listing results by relevance alone does not work, as searches carried out on structured databases will always be 100% relevant or they would not be displayed. Displaying by application searched places the integration and interpretation load on the searcher. There is no easy answer, and a substantial investment in usability testing will not only be necessary at the outset, but also on a continuing basis as the pattern of search queries settles down.

A major issue for anyone carrying out a search is the extent to which they feel able to assess the value of the content associated with each hit. This is not the same as relevance. Relevance is a mathematical analysis of the content, and a searcher may decide to use an item because the source of the content is trusted even if the document does not have the optimum relevance.

The budget challenge

Determining the budget for an enterprise-level implementation is far from easy. Although the basic elements are those set out in Chapter 4, there is much less information available at the outset about the scope of the implementation in terms of the number of servers, applications, document volumes and use levels. Even if the core licence costs can be broadly quantified, the level of the professional services support required to carry out the implementation requires very careful analysis. There may also be a need to add in new hardware and network management equipment, and the budgets for these may be held within an individual country or subsidiary. The issues of how best to manage the timing of software upgrades and capital investment in new equipment may take some time to resolve.

Federated search

It is inevitable in most enterprises that there will be search functionality embedded in business applications as an enterprise resource planning application, as well as a number of intranet search applications, especially where the company is highly decentralized. The ideal solution would be to provide a federated search solution that enables the user to have a consistent experience in terms of the desktop, and to be able to carry out searches in which the execution of a query against any of these applications is optimized for both the query and the application. The requirement for federated search is being driven to a significant extent by a number of factors, of which the primary ones are:

- locating all documents and other files associated with a particular transaction where there is a need to demonstrate legal compliance
- reducing the need to train users in a range of different search applications when their use of any specific application may be quite limited
- reducing the IT and related support requirements from having to manage multiple search platforms.

Federated search solutions are now emerging from both the major IT vendors such as IBM and Oracle, and also from search engine vendors that include Autonomy, Endeca, Fast Search, Inxight and Vivisimo. The challenges that they have to overcome are as follows:

- **Result presentation variability** Each application may present search results in radically different formats, with or without information explaining why an item was included, or how they were ranked. Merely merging results sets in some linear form is not going to be much assistance to the user. One option might be to present the results as a scrolling page of the results from different servers or search applications, and let the user do the selection and integration, but this can be time-consuming.

- **Results management** A search may result in a very large number of results, but many of these may be duplicate documents. Should all the duplicates be presented to the user? Although many search engines, especially those using a vector space algorithm, claim to be able to de-duplicate, the question in the user's mind will always be the basis on which the de-duplication has been carried out.
- **Ranking algorithms** In order to merge results sets there needs to be a translation of the relevance rankings from results sets that rank items similarly and order the results list similarly, or those that modify the results set so that it conforms to a particular set of formatting and ranking characteristics. It is often difficult to determine exactly how a search engine selects one document over another.
- **Language management** The diversity of languages is difficult enough to handle in a single search engine, but becomes much more difficult in a federated search application.
- **Site selection** Some users may want to search every available site, until they discover that some sites are down and that others contain nothing remotely related to their query. Providing the user with a mechanism to preselect a subset of searchable indexes saves time and computing resources. Think of it as the first step in refining a search.
- **System delays** Because searchable sites can be anywhere in the world, response times can vary dramatically. As merging results is difficult and time-consuming, sites that are slow to respond or that fail to respond at all must be abandoned within a reasonable period. But this needs to be reported to the user, along with information that will allow them to determine whether or not to try the site again or to remove it from the list of sites to search.

Ten steps to implementing enterprise search

The ten steps in the process of implementing enterprise search are:

Step 1 Who are the stakeholders?
Step 2 What will be the benefits to the business?
Step 3 What are the technology issues?
Step 4 What happens to the existing search applications?
Step 5 Examine the implementation options
Step 6 Work up a risk analysis
Step 7 Select a vendor or upgrade an existing one
Step 8 Test for performance and relevance
Step 9 Train and support searchers
Step 10 Have a fallback strategy.

Step 1 Who are the stakeholders?

With enterprise search this is not just a question of identifying the needs of users. At this level, search can become an applications integration platform, and this may have implications for other business applications, ranging from a customer management system to a business intelligence system. There was a view (until Microsoft accomplished it) that the company that owned the desktop would also end up being the filter through which all other applications were delivered. Search presents a similar opportunity, or challenge, depending on which side of the divide a particular stakeholder sits.

Identifying these stakeholders can be difficult. Although an IT manager should have a good view of current and planned projects, it is also important to understand the plans of business managers, compliance managers and risk managers, as well as finance managers.

Step 2 What will be the benefits to the business?

The challenge here is that the various stakeholders might have very different views of how enterprise search could benefit the business, ranging from compliance audits to enhancing innovation and knowledge transfer. Integrating these into a single business plan is not going to be easy, and it will take time to bring all relevant stakeholders into a consensus, no matter how senior the sponsor of the project.

Step 3 What are the technology issues?

The range of technology issues is also going to be more complex. For an organization working across several time zones, server downtime for maintenance may start to become an issue. If the search engine has to index files on remote servers there needs to be enough bandwidth to ensure that this process is not too prolonged, or that indexing is fully complete and has to be restarted. Upgrades will almost certainly be taking place to one or more enterprise applications at any one time, and these need to be taken into account in the scheduling.

Step 4 What happens to the existing search applications?

Many of the current applications will already have some degree of search functionality. There are three options:

1. Retain the full functionality for core users, and provide others with access through a federated search option.
2. Extend the search functionality of the application to be the enterprise search solution. This is certainly an option with some of the enterprise-level document management applications.
3. Decommission the current search application and allow the enterprise search solution to provide search.

Step 5 Examine the implementation options

There is unlikely to be an immediately obvious implementation path, no matter which of the three options is considered. Integrating any other application will be dependent not only on work that needs to be carried out with the enterprise search solution, but also any upgrades or heavy business requirements on other applications.

This is where the initial work with stakeholders (Step 1) pays off. However, there is unlikely to be an obvious implementation option. All the critical dependencies need to be established, taking into account resource issues, information systems architecture upgrades, and product development roadmaps from the search software vendors. The end result will probably be a Gantt chart of considerable complexity that will need not only refinement at the start, but constant revisions as the implementation proceeds.

One approach might be to develop a dot.version approach that all software vendors use for their product releases:

1.1 Provide enhanced intranet search using the enterprise search solution (ESS).
1.2.1 Extend ESS to cover US SharePoint applications.
1.2.2 Extend ESS to cover European SharePoint applications.
1.3 Index Microsoft Exchange e-mail servers.
1.4 Extend ESS to document management applications.

Some of the steps may be quite small, but the benefits of this approach are that:

- It helps the search implementation team to look at the implementation options in an appropriate level of detail.
- Implementation communication is enhanced because reference can be made to a numeric version, which is especially important in multilingual applications.
- If it becomes clear that a particular implementation stage needs to be undertaken in a series of substeps, then this can be denoted by a three-level number replacing the two-level number, as shown above.

Step 6 Work up a risk analysis

A good risk analysis is always of value in a search implementation, but is absolutely critical in implementing an enterprise solution to meet the expectations of the various stakeholders. Constructing the original register is less than half the challenge. The risks must be reviewed on an agreed basis, and the resources (and organizational commitment) have to be there to take avoiding action.

Step 7 Select a vendor or upgrade an existing one

In the case of intranet and website search there is currently a range of specialized software vendors who can provide solutions. At an enterprise level the major IT vendors come into play, notably IBM and Oracle, and also SAP, enterprise portal vendors such as BEA, and even enterprise document management vendors such as EMC Documentum and Open Text. The result is that there is much more likely to be an incumbent supplier who would wish to provide the enterprise search solution, and who, because of the scale of the investment they have already made in developing the customer relationship, will be able to offer good value for money and (at least in theory) a smooth implementation plan.

Another option in many organizations is to use the incumbent systems integrator or outsourcing company. Many of these companies have channel partner arrangements with a small number of search companies, mainly to ensure that their integration expertise does not have to accommodate too many different products. The result is that there may not be as full a choice of search solution as the organization might suppose. Over the last couple of years most Microsoft partners would invariably offer Mondosoft as the search solution because it works well on a .NET platform, but now SharePoint 2007 is an obvious option. It should also be noted that at present few systems integrators have implemented enterprise search solutions.

Step 8 Test for performance and relevance

The importance of establishing and monitoring system performance parameters cannot be overstated. Users may accept a two-second delay in the response from a finance application, but will be much more critical of a search solution. Especially in an enterprise environment there may need to be a number of search refinement steps, and if there is a perception that time will be wasted waiting for the system to respond, then use will diminish rapidly and permanently.

As mentioned above, the effectiveness of the search process in terms of delivering relevant documents also needs to be managed with care and a good sense of why particular users may be experiencing problems.

Step 9 Train and support searchers

It does not take much effort to make searching a website or intranet fairly intuitive. Indeed, if users of either have to be trained, then the cause is lost from the start! Because of the heterogeneous nature of the content to be searched and the searches that are likely to be carried out, there will be a need to provide training, helpdesk support, and contextual help on the search engine itself.

Step 10 Have a fallback strategy

Implementing enterprise-level search is a challenging project, primarily because the implementation team may only have a limited amount of input into the choices being made for other applications, in terms of either the software being used or when upgrades will be undertaken. Commitment to a cast-in-stone implementation plan is not to be recommended. The fallback strategy should come directly out of the risk assessment in Step 6. The work in Step 6 will tend to focus on some specifics (perhaps a server or network upgrade), but this needs to be extended in Step 10 to show what the trigger points might be for not continuing with the implementation beyond certain specific stages.

Chapter 12
Multilingual search

In this chapter:

- Why multilingual search is so difficult
- The value of Unicode
- The problems of transliteration

Searching the Tower of Babel

The issues concerning searching in multiple languages are often poorly understood, and yet the need to be able to do so is going to be increasingly important. Research from Byte Level Research (http://bytelevel.com) indicates that the majority of internet users are not native-English speakers.

From the perspective of website search, this means that there may be a considerable number of visitors searching the site who may have only a limited range of synonyms and linguistic awareness. This is not just on a cross-national basis. It is estimated that over 300 languages are spoken in London alone, though this is probably the most linguistically diverse city in the world. Clearly, in the period up to the 2008 Olympic Games, the growth in Chinese users is considerable.

The management of multiple languages also needs to be carefully considered in the enterprise environment. Just because an organization has English as its global corporate language does not mean to say that all documents will be in English. Documents relating to staff contracts and policies, and contracts with local suppliers, will invariably be in local languages. Patents and other legal documents will also be in more than one language, and if any one individual user is to have global access to the resources of the organization, the problems of how to search in a language-independent way as regards both the language skills of the searcher and the languages of the documents need to be addressed.

Searching multiple languages

Many search engines claim to be able to search in multiple languages, but care must be taken over just what this means. It usually means that the search engine can parse a document written in a wide range of languages, create an index, and then run a query against that index to present a number of relevant documents. Although not easy to undertake, this is now quite well developed technology and uses Unicode to convert a language to a standardized (or rather normalized) format. This enables a search to be carried out using a query in the destination language. The ideal is for any searcher to be able to use their own language as the query (source) language and for the search engine to be able to match the query against destination languages. This can only be done with a multilingual synonym directory against which any given term is matched, undertaking, in effect, a federated search.

One of the initial problems is to make sure that the language is correctly recognized. In an enterprise environment there may not only be documents on the same server that are written in different languages (for example English and Arabic), but in addition a document may be written in English and then contain text (perhaps from an official document) in Arabic. The document may also have been written on wordprocessing software that has been developed for Arabic users, and the file extension may not be among those supported by the search software. Arabic is a good example of another problem, in that there are many different variants of Arabic, so that the script used in Saudi Arabia is slightly different from that used in Iran and Iraq.

Unicode

The Unicode standard is a character coding system designed to support the worldwide interchange, processing and display of the written texts of the diverse languages and technical disciplines of the modern world. It supports classical and historical texts of many written languages, including the European alphabetic scripts, Middle Eastern right-to-left scripts, and many scripts of Asia.

The current version of the Unicode standard is version 5.0.0, which was released in 2006 and is a significant revision of the standard. It defines what the character is in code terms but does not say how it will be represented as what is called a glyph, so it is format neutral. It does distinguish between upper- and lower-case letters, however. Some characters have more than one encoding, so that the mathematical symbol *pi* has a different coding from the letter *pi* used in a Greek word.

There are three levels of coding: UTF-8 (often used for HTML files), UTF-16 and UTF-32. Full details of these can be found on the website of the Unicode Consortium.[1] The greatest challenges are presented by Chinese, Japanese, Korean and Vietnamese, all languages from countries with a major economic impact on world trade. Collectively these are known as the CJKV languages.[2]

Identifying index terms

The first challenge for the search engine is to identify the words that need to be indexed. This is a major issue for languages such as Japanese, Chinese and Korean, which have no spaces between 'words'. One approach is called the 'N-gram' technique. This divides a sequence of characters into segments that are *n* characters in length - usually two or three. The same process is used for the query, and then a match is performed against the character string sets generated from the analysis of the document. There are two problems with this approach. The first is that the semantic meaning of the word is lost, and so synonym matching is impossible. The second is that the size of the index is substantially greater than the number of keywords, which has implications for server capacity and search performance. The third issue is that stemming is very difficult to manage.

The second approach is to use morphological analysis, which uses language dictionaries and a set of rules about the way in which words, phrases and sentences are constructed in each language. This results in much smaller index volumes and better search results, but is much more complex to develop and implement, and so comes at a higher price.

As with so many aspects of specifying a search engine, it is important to be absolutely clear which languages the organization may wish to search, and how well a search engine solution will be able to manage those languages. Of the European languages, Greek presents special challenges because of the 24-character alphabet against the norm of 26. At the time of writing, Ultraseek (for example) has language modules for most of the major European languages but not for Greek. Polish and some other languages (Croatian is a good example) are poorly supported in general by search engines. Probably the ultimate challenge is Azerbaijani, which can be written in both Cyrillic and Arabic scripts.

Transliteration of names

One of the major problems in searching across multiple languages is the way in which the names of authors or employees are presented. This is a particular problem in Arabic, where the construction of a person's name is quite complex. This can often result in a long name which the person concerned may well then shorten for use within either the organization or a local office. The problem also arises in Spain and Portugal, where people have at least two surnames, one inherited from the father, the other from the mother. However, in Spain and most Spanish-speaking countries the father's surname is written before the mother's. In Portugal and Brazil the father's surname is in most cases placed after the mother's.

As a result, searching for documents written by specific employees, or for information about those employees, requires an awareness of the way in which the employee concerned may truncate or transliterate their name. An employee with an Arabic name may prefer to use their full name while working on a project in an Arabic-speaking country, but use a more colloquial form when working in Europe. For example, Hassan al-Ghobashy could be listed in the corporate telephone directory under A, E or G:

AL-GHOBASHY Hassan
EL-GHOBASHY Hassan
GHOBASHY Hassan al-

One of the many problems with Arabic is that only eight Arabic letters have a clear equivalent in the Roman alphabet: B, F, K, L, M, N, R and Z.[3]

The problems are even more challenging in China, where although there are over 500 family names there are fewer than 100 in common use. Considerable attention has to be paid to the given name or names, which are written after the family name. As is the case with Arabic names, the person may reverse the order of presentation when dealing with countries with a given name - family name sequence, but because most of us are not familiar with Chinese family names no indicator is given of which is used.

Even with European names there is the requirement to adapt names in languages such as German in order to work with text editors and ASCII applications such as plain text e-mail. Searching for information about a Frau Koehner requires the search engine to be instructed to search for both Koehner and Köhner.

Phonetic problems also arise. If someone is asked to find information on work by Qiao Qiao Chang, the person asking for the work to be carried out, who knows the correct pronunciation, will pronounce the name as 'Chow Chow'. Another possible pronunciation might be Key-ow Key-ow, and this again will give rise to query management issues.

The problem also extends to geographic names. The city of Cologne does not exist, but the city of Köln does. Google does a good job of offering a synonym dictionary, but there are still 4 million more hits for 'Cologne city' than there are for 'Köln city'.

There are also national variations of transliteration. The former Soviet President Yeltsin is a pronounceable transliteration of Ельцин, the formal English transliteration being Elt'sin. In a French newpaper the name might be transliterated as either Eltsine or Yeltsine. Another example of the impact of French transliteration is that the composer Tchaikovsky is rendered as Chaikovsky. These rules are often built into search engines, but it is essential to check that any specific words that might be in common use in an organization, or by visitors to a site, are identified and suitable synonyms suggested or used.

A good example of Arabic transliteration is that there are at least 87 different ways of writing the name of the Libyan President Muammar el Gaddafi.[4]

All these issues may, on their own, seem to be rather pedantic, but in a multilingual world will become increasingly important in delivering effective search. English speakers in particular are often poorly aware of the implications of language.[5]

Understanding the language search options

The way in which search engine vendors provide solutions to these problems varies widely, and is often not explicitly spelt out on the websites. The FAQ section of one search engine vendor contains the following statement:

> **Do you support queries across multiple languages?**
> Yes. All documents regardless of identified language may be stored within an index. Searches against the index may return results across the index, or filtered by language as desired. Also note that a result page can for instance contain search results in different languages (with corresponding character encodings) such as Arabic, Japanese and English displayed in their original character encoding. As another example, a given document can contain text in multiple languages and corresponding character encodings and you can still search on all of these at the same time.

This rather skirts round the issue, and is typical of the current lack of clarity in the industry. Most vendors do not have their own linguistic engine but use the technology developed by companies such as Basis Technology (www.basis-tech.com) and Teregram (www.teregram.com). Each vendor then builds their own solution around these specialized modules. Autonomy uses a different approach, citing that its Dynamic Reasoning Engine treats words as abstract symbols of meaning deriving its understanding through the context of their occurrence rather than a rigid definition of the language grammar.[6]

As with so many aspects of implementing search applications, the best route to meeting expectations is to be absolutely certain what those expectations are, and then to select a vendor on the basis of this analysis.

References

1 www.unicode.org.
2 Lunde, K. (1999) CJKV Information Processing, Sebastopol CA, O'Reilly Publishing, www.oreilly.com.
3 www.al-bab.com/arab/language/roman1.htm.
4 www.theglobalist.com/DBWeb/StoryId.aspx?StoryId=5089.
5 www.xrce.xerox.com/competencies/content-analysis/arabic/info/romanization.html.
6 Autonomy (2006) Autonomy Overview 2006, Autonomy Corp., 20, www.autonomy.com.

Chapter 13

Future directions

In this chapter:

- What direction will the search industry take?
- How important is innovation by Google and Microsoft?
- Convergence of search and business intelligence
- Social software and search

One of the themes of this book has been the need to plan ahead, to assess what the needs of the organization will be in the years to come, so that the best strategic fit can be made between the requirements of the organization and the implementation of a search engine, whether for a website, the desktop, one or more intranets, or for enterprise-wide search. This chapter takes the risky approach of trying to suggest the directions that search technology will take in the future. A reader looking at this chapter even a year or so after publication may well be amused rather than informed.

Having spent over ten years in the business of high-technology market forecasting I look back on some of the reports that I wrote over that time and can now scarcely credit the astounding rate of progress that has been achieved, especially in the area of price-performance.

So, here are some predictions for the future, in the hope that, if nothing else, they will make you, the reader, focus on what is happening in the areas I have highlighted, and draw your own interpretation and vision.

Search is going to be a big business

Most IT markets grow on an S-curve, with a number of early adopters who then act as validation for the technology and its initial applications. After that there is a more general uptake, which is rarely truly exponential. Even though computer-based search has been available for over 40 years, its adoption by organizations is still in the very early stages. We are still at the very beginning of the S-curve, and the main reason for this is not that the technology did not work but that there was no identifiable market.

Now that market is beginning to exist. The advent of content management software to enable websites to be created and managed more easily, the total inability of organizations to find anything in e-mail servers, the widespread use of shared drives, the ubiquity of Microsoft SharePoint and the demands for compliance solutions are just a few of the drivers for this market.

It is difficult to gain any quantitative sense of the current installed base of search software, excluding those organizations that have enterprise platforms from companies such as IBM, Microsoft (i.e. SharePoint Portal) and SAP where search is bundled in. As far as the independent search vendors are concerned, the installed base is probably no more than 100,000 organization sites, including websites. Open source solutions for websites are also excluded from this total. Even if this total is low by an order of magnitude, the market is currently small but capable of immense growth. The intranet installed base in the UK alone is probably around 300,000 at a minimum. There is therefore every reason for suppliers of search products of all types to put as much investment as possible into taking advantage of this market.

Search software vendors will continue to show low profitability

This investment will come at a cost. There is still a lot of ignorance about search, and so the lead time to sell to a new customer is quite high. This is one reason why many vendors are encouraging potential customers to download software for a pilot trial, hoping to reduce the sales effort and to lock in a customer who is so impressed with what they have downloaded that they make no effort to see whether it is in fact the best fit for purpose.

The price-points for search are decreasing as new entrants seemingly offer everything for a low price, and the major vendors have to move to lower their licence fees. This will put pressure on all vendors to maintain their profitability at a level that is adequate to fund the research costs involved, not just in developing novel software but in continuing to enhance the software ahead of customer requirements.

Compared to content management software, the research resources required for search are significantly greater because of the complexity of the systems, as set out in Chapter 2. As of 31 May 2005 (and before the acquisition by Autonomy) Verity had a total of 554 employees, of whom 160 were in research and development. Verity is presented here just as an example, primarily because it is one of the few search vendors that is a public company and so has to file accounts.

The web will continue to stimulate search innovation

Looking at the rate of product release, and in particular the advent of OneBox and the growth of channel partner relationships worldwide, Google is clearly commited to the search appliance business. This is in many respects a good thing, as Google has made enterprise search a respectable business. Google never releases market shipment figures, which is probably just as well, as many other vendors would have sleepless nights. However, if Google is really going to succeed in the enterprise market it will have to invest in customer support at the same level as it does in search technology. Providing a helpdesk service based on e-mail for a mission-critical product such as search is not going to be adequate, and yet the price of the search appliances is almost too low to be able to enhance customer support.

Microsoft has not had a great deal to offer in the search market, which is why Mondosoft has done well out of its relationship with Microsoft, with Steve Ballmer of Microsoft citing Mondosoft as one of its five essential technology partners. At the 2006 World Partner Conference the progress that Microsoft was making on incorporating better search into its products was the first of the highlight announcements during Ballmer's initial presentation.[1] This will, of course, put pressure on the companies that have been making a good business out of adding better search functionality to SharePoint servers.

In general, the public web space is where search innovations are going to be seen first, because of market scale and demand. For example, Powerset (www.powerset.com) plans to offer natural language search functionality, something that CEO Barney Pell has been writing about in his blog (www.barneypell.com/) for some time. Interestingly Pell plans to make use of Amazon's Elastic Compute Cloud technology, just one of the web service offerings that Amazon has developed over the last few years as an outcome of its website development (http://aws.amazon.com).

CMS and search will become better integrated

Many organizations have found to their cost that most CMS products do not contain an effective search engine, often relying on an OEM version of Verity. Increasingly, CMS vendors and the search vendors will realize that they should be working in tandem. The CMS vendors have an installed base an order of magnitude and more than the search vendors, so CMS represents a good route to market. The integration of the Mondosoft search engine with Sitecore CMS product, announced in mid-2006, is a good example. It will be interesting to see whether Oracle starts to ship its enterprise search software with its Stellent CMS product range, acquired at the end of 2006.

Search solutions that work across semistructured and structured data will be much in demand

Even though there is a view that companies do not make use of the value of the information on semistructured text files, the same is also true of structured databases, where retrieval is often locked in to standard calls to the database. There is a clear requirement to be able to search across both types of resource, even in the smallest of companies, as sales staff in particular try to find out what is available in Word documents, e-mails and sales ledgers to build up a corporate perspective of a customer. This is not a trivial problem to solve because of the fundamental principles of fully normalized relational databases, but it is likely that solutions will emerge in the very near future.

Business intelligence and search will converge

Because of this need to search across two different data types, the major business intelligence software vendors, such as Cognos, Business Objects, Information Builders and Microstrategy, will be looking at search functionality as a competitive advantage. Cognos is already partnering with Google for the OneBox product. These large and generally profitable companies could be in the market for search software vendors. The annual revenues of Cognos are around $1bn, which is larger than the total search software market. Text mining is also a component of business intelligence, and in late 2006 there was an announcement that Endeca (faceted navigation) and Clarabridge (data mining) were going to collaborate on developing the business intelligence market sector.

Federated search will continue to improve, because it has to

The need to be able to integrate searches carried out across multiple search engines and/or repositories will grow in importance. Portal vendors in particular need good federated search capability, and SAP is just one example, as it starts to position its TREX search product as a wider enterprise search engine rather than restricting it to just searching SAP repositories. Oracle has considerable portal experience and a renewed commitment to search through secure enterprise search. BEA is also playing a lot of attention to search, and of course Microsoft is re-entering the portal business with a much improved SharePoint product.

Visualization software will improve rapidly

Early attempts to provide a visual representation of search results have not been all that successful, but with the advent of Web 2.0 technologies and the need to make sense of federated search results there will a considerable amount of product innovation, for example the software developed by Groxis (www.groxis.com).

There will be substantial progress in searching single and sequential images

This is an area where Autonomy has invested significantly in its Virage search product, and Google is also potentially a major player, especially following the partnership with Intel that was announced in early 2006. With the growth of image-sharing sites such as Flickr the market demand for image search is going to grow rapidly, and among the companies seeking to offer solutions are Tiltomo (www.tiltomo.com) and Like (www.like.com/). Another catalyst in the development of video searching is the need to scan and index closed-circuit television images for security purposes.

Social tagging will come to search

Social tagging, which started with Delicious and Flickr, has now become a major element of the Web 2.0 spectrum. The search industry is now starting to explore social tagging. Collarity (www.collarity.com) is one entrant to this area, and in mid-2006 portal vendor BEA launched Project Graffiti. Graffiti allows users to browse or search the Graffiti indexed collection, applying content labels, or 'tagging' documents the system will track for them individually. The system creates personal or custom views of information, and suggests content that may be useful to an individual user based on a combination of usage patterns, analytics and activity tagging. Another development in this area is the launch of Kshoni as a search product for collaborative work groups.

Third-party information vendors will have to review their position on search

One major issue with intranet and enterprise search is that it is very difficult for users to search external information resources, such as Factiva or Lexis

Nexis, using the enterprise search solution. Many information services vendors do push content into organizational repositories, but this assumes that the organization can define its information requirements. Being able to search the entire repository of, say, Factiva in the case of a hostile bid could be valuable. There are some technical and cost factors to be addressed, but so far there has been little discussion of the benefits and issues.

Reference

1 www.microsoft.com/presspass/exec/steve/2006/07-11WPC2006.mspx.

Appendix
Search software vendors

In this section:

Brief profiles have been provided of nearly 40 search vendors. This is not intended to be a comprehensive list of all vendors, nor does it imply any endorsement by the author or Intranet Focus Ltd. The companies with the notation ESR are those listed in the 2006 edition of the CMS Watch Enterprise Search Report.

Active Navigation
www.activenavigation.com
HQ: Southampton, UK

Initially founded under the name Multicosm Ltd, Active Navigation has its roots in the research carried out at the University of Southampton into the structure of navigation, innovative models of hypertext, and the thematic analysis of text using linguistic and statistical techniques. The company is privately owned.

Arikus
www.arikus.com
HQ: Toronto, Canada

Arikus was set up in 1997 as an information management consultancy. The core of the Arikus products is the Arikus Information Refinery Engine, AIRE. The software is priced very competitively, with an enterprise licence for up to 3 million documents being priced at $19,995. There is also a developer version for incorporation into specific enterprise applications.

Atomz (ESR)
www.websidestory.com
HQ: San Diego, California, USA

Atomz was the trading name of Avivo corporation, which was founded in 1996 with the objective of offering outsourced content management solutions. It moved into search solutions and in February 2005. was acquired by WebSideStory. The revenues of WebSideStory are around $70m.

Autonomy Corporation (ESR)
www.autonomy.com
HQ: Cambridge, UK

Autonomy was founded by Dr Michael Lynch OBE and Richard Gaunt in 1996 as a means of commercializing the work that they had carried out on the use of Bayesian statistics to underpin pattern recognition as a search technology. In 2005 the company acquired Verity Inc. for $502m, and in so doing became the largest search-specific software vendor. Autonomy had ready acquired etalk Corp. Autonomy is continuing to support all current versions of K2, as well as developing the latest and future generations of K2, to be known as IDOL K2. The company has stated that it intends to continue support of K2, and that the first release (K2 IDOL 7) will be usable by customers at their discretion, either as a standalone product or in a new mode running as a part of the IDOL infrastructure.

BA-Insight
www.ba-insight.net
HQ: White Plains, New York, USA

BA-Insight was established in 2003 and offers the Longitude search appliance to enhance the performance of Microsoft SharePoint servers. The company is privately owned. The three founders worked together at the French company Suez on the development of search applications.

Blossom (ESR)
www.blossom.com
HQ: Brookline, Massachusetts, USA

Blossom Software was incorporated in 2000 to commercialize internet agent technology developed by one of its founders in the late 1990s. Initially the company offered hosted web search services, but more recently has offered InSearch as a downloadable intranet search application which is leased on an annual basis. The company also offers an Enterprise Search product, but this is in fact a hosted search product for customers that have multiple websites.

BrightPlanet
www.brightplanet.com
Sioux Falls, South Dakota, USA

BrightPlanet has developed a range of specialized applications that can be integrated into third-party software products. These include the Deep Query Manager content discovery, harvesting, management and analysis platform for documents from the internet, internal intranets and/or file systems.

Convera Corporation (ESR)
www.convera.com
HQ: Vienna, Virginia, USA

The history of Convera is a complex one: Convera Corporation was established through the combination on 21 December 2000 of the former Excalibur Technologies Corporation and Intel Corporation's Interactive Media Services division. Currently 47% of the shares are held by Allen and

Company, a major US investment bank. The company offers its RetrievalWare product as an enterprise search solution, but is increasingly focusing its resources on the development of Excalibur as a private label search service for online publishers and similar organizations.

Copernic
www.copernic.com
HQ: Quebec, Canada

The Copernic range of products was initially based on search technology developed by Agents Technologies Corporation, which was founded in Quebec in the mid-1990s. In late 2005 Copernic was acquired by Mamma.com Inc, a web meta-search service vendor that was founded in 1996. Several senior directors of Copernic joined the Board of Directors of Mamma.com Inc. In July 2006 the company announced its Copernic Desktop Search (CDS) Private Branding Program for ISPs and major portals.

Coveo Solutions Inc. (ESR)
www.coveo.com
HQ: Quebec, Canada

Coveo was spun out of Copernic in October 2004 to commercialize the Copernic search technology in the enterprise market. Although no revenue information is released, in May 2006 Coveo announced a 400% increase in revenue during the company's last financial year. As well as a general enterprise search product the company also offers a specialized version of its software for Microsoft SharePoint applications.

CrownPeak
www.crownpeak.com
HQ: Los Angeles, California, USA

CrownPeak was established in January 2001 to provide hosted website management services. These now include hosted search capabilities. The pricing is based on the volume of content, the number of sites, and the number of searches carried out.

Dieselpoint

www.dieselpoint.com

HQ: Chicago, Illinois, USA

Dieselpoint released the initial version of its enterprise search engine in 2000. The search engine is written entirely in Java, and indexes are stored in a Dieselpoint-proprietary file format.

dtSearch (ESR)

www.dtsearch.com

HQ: Bethesda, Maryland, USA

The company started research and development in text retrieval in 1988 and began marketing the first dtSearch product in the first quarter of that year. The company is run by its founder, David Thede. The pricing model is based on the number of users. A feature of the software is the support for a range of relevance models.

EasyAsk

www.easyask.com

HQ: Bedford, Maryland, USA

EasyAsk was founded in 1994 by Dr Larry Harris, a computational linguistics professor at Dartmouth College. The company was acquired in May 2005 by Progress Software Corporation, a $500m revenue software and services company.

Endeca (ESR)

www.endeca.com

HQ: Cambridge, Massachusetts, USA

Endeca was founded by Steve Papa (formerly with Inktomi) in 1999. As with many other search companies, revenue information is not disclosed, but in May 2006 the company announced that revenues had increased by 85% for the first quarter of the financial year compared to the previous year. The Endeca Information Access Platform is based on a patented meta-relational architecture, powered by MDEX Engine™ to provide what the company styles guided navigation.

Engenium

www.engenium.com
HQ: Dallas, Texas, USA

Engenium was founded in 1998 and offers the Semetric and Autometric conceptual search and document clustering engines that use sophisticated semantic analysis to search structured and unstructured information. The company is privately owned.

Entopia

www.entopia.com
HQ: Haifa, Israel

This company went out of business in late 2006.

Exalead

www.exalead.com
HQ: Paris, France

François Bourdoncle co-founded Exalead in 2000 with Patrice Bertin, the company's chief technology officer, with whom he had worked on the LiveTopics project for AltaVista. The objective of the company is to offer a unified technology platform for desktop, intranet and web search using 64-bit computing technology, and to be the major competitor to Google. A major investor in Exalead is the French investment group Qualis.

Fast Search (ESR)

www.fastsearch.com
HQ: Oslo, Norway

John Marcus Lervik was studying digital signal processing at the Norwegian University of Science and Technology in Trondheim, and in 1999 Lervik and initial business partner Espen Brandin formed Fast Search. Over the last five years it has become the second largest search software vendor after Autonomy, with revenues in excess of $120m and with over 600 employees. Over the last year the ownership of Fast has come under scrutiny, as the company extracted itself from the stake that Norwegian company Opticom had in the company as a result of its initial investment in Fast.

Funnelback (ESR)
http://funnelback.com
HQ: Canberra, Australia

The company was founded in 1998 by Dr David Hawking, a world leader in information retrieval, to commercialize the P@noptic (more commonly written as Panoptic) search software developed at the Commonwealth Scientific and Industrial Research Organization (CSIRO), Clayton South, Australia. The company was spun off from CSIRO in February 2006. One of the features of the product is a highly customizable user interface.

Google (ESR)
www.google.com
HQ: Mountain View, California, USA

(See pages 34-35)

Groxis.com
www.groxis.com
HQ: San Francisco, California, USA

Groxis was founded in 2001 and offers Grokker as a federated web-based search product that can search both web resources and enterprise files, presenting the results using visualization technology. Grokker is also positioned as an add-on to search appliances, in particular the Google Search Appliance, and has also been integrated within the Fast Search product.

IBM (ESR)
www-306.ibm.com/software/sw-bycategory/subcategory/SWB40.html

(See pages 36-37)

Innerprise (ESR)
www.innerprise.net
HQ: Scottsdale, Arizona

Innerprise was founded in 1998 and offers both a low-cost .NET search engine and a hosted search service for websites.

Inquira (ESR)

www.inquira.com

HQ: San Bruno, California, USA

The company was founded in 2002 by Michael Murphy and Ed Cooper, who has an extensive background in computational linguistics and artificial intelligence theory. While he was a PhD student, Cooper conceived of and led the OnPoint project, a web-based information retrieval system with a natural language interface, and worked at IBM's Santa Teresa Laboratory on natural language text retrieval-related projects, along with Brian Slivak, another InQuira executive. The key element of the range of Inquira products is a semantic processing engine.

Interse

www.interse.com

HQ: Copenhagen, Denmark

Interse specializes in search solutions for Microsoft applications, in particular Microsoft SharePoint with its iBox software. The company is privately owned, with a significant stake held by Nordic Venture Partners.

Inxight Software

www.inxight.com

HQ: Sunnyvale, California, USA

Inxight was founded in 1997 as a spin-off from Xerox PARC, and focuses on federated search and high-fidelity extraction technology. It has a wide range of visualization products, including StarTree, TableLens and TimeWall.

Isys Search (ESR)

www.isys-search.com

HQ: Sydney, Australia

Ian Davies, the Managing Director of Isys Search, founded in company in Sydney, Australia, in 1988. The company claims to have over 16,000 customers, which is probably the largest customer base of any of the search software vendors. One of the primary selling points of Isys has always been speed and ease of implementation.

Kaidara
www.kaidara.com
HQ: Paris and Los Altos, USA

Kaidara was founded in 2001 with investments from both French and US sources. The company focuses on discovering patterns in the responses received by organisations through customer feedback and call centre operations.

Knova Software
www.knova.com
HQ: Cupertino, California

Knova Software, Inc. was created by the merger in 2005 of Kanisa (a pioneer of service resolution management applications) and ServiceWare, which offered knowledge management solutions for service and support applications. It is one of the few publicly-traded search vendors. These two call centre applications have now been merged in the Knova 7 product range.

Kshoni

See Voltix below.

Lextek
www.lextek.com
HQ: Provo, Utah, USA

Lextek International was founded in 1993 and specializes in advanced information retrieval and natural language processing technology, with a particular focus on linguistic technologies. As well as its Onix full text retrieval software, one of the products offered by the company is a language identifier which can recognize over 260 different languages.

Lucene
http://apache.lucene.org
HQ: Forest Hill MD, USA

Lucene is the leading open source search engine, and as well as being used in native mode is also widely used as the core search module by other vendors, such as the Alfresco document management software and the Searchblox search application (see below). It was written by Doug Nutting in 1997 and 1998. Nutting also wrote Nutch, which adds web crawlers and some additional search functionality to the Lucene core engine. Nutch was supported by Yahoo!, and Doug Nutting joined Yahoo! in 2006.

Mercado Software
www.mercado.com
HQ: Pleasanton, California

Mecardo Software specializes in search solutions for e-commerce and business-to-business applications. One of the core elements of these solutions is the UniClass categorization engine, which automatically extracts attributes from unstructured product information, normalizes those attributes and classifies the products into a unified taxonomy.

Microsoft (ESR)
www.microsoft.com

(See pages 37-38)

Mondosoft (ESR)
www.mondosoft.com
HQ: Copenhagen, Denmark

Mondosoft was founded in 1998 by Laust Sondergaard, a co-founder of Mondo A/S, the agency that produced Denmark's first commercial website. The company specializes in supporting Microsoft implementations. MondoSearch is an advanced, multilingual search engine that helps users quickly find relevant data across the enterprise and BehaviorTracking is an analytical reporting tool that provides critical information on the search activity and visitor behaviour on a website. The company is privately held. In February 2006 Mondosoft acquired Navigo Systems A/S, a privately held search and taxonomy software provider specializing in optimizing Microsoft SharePoint solutions through its Ontolica product.

Nervana

www.nervana.com
HQ: Bellevue, Washington, USA

Nervana's technology constructs semantic maps of source documents and ranks and groups retrieved documents according to how well they match semantic maps of user queries and how well they fit user-specified knowledge contexts. The technology was developed by Nosa Omoigui, the President of Nervana, who was formerly at Microsoft. The company specializes in search solutions for the pharmaceutical industry.

Northern Light

www.northernlight.com
HQ: Cambridge, Massachusetts, USA

Northern Light was established in 1996, initially as an innovative public web search engine that was one of the first to use clustering as a means of enhancing search performance. The company offers a range of search products, including an enterprise search application, and makes a very public disclosure of its pricing policies on its website. The search software only runs on Linux.

Nutch

See Lucene (above).

Oracle (ESR)

www.oracle.com

(See page 38)

PolySpot

www.polyspot.com
HQ: Paris

Polyspot was established in 2006 from the European operations of Triplehop Technologies. The Matchpoint technology developed by Triplehop was acquired by Oracle in 2005. Polyspot has been set up to exploit other Triplehop technologies, and the company has now released a low-cost enterprise search application.

Recommind

www.recommind.com
HQ: San Francisco, California, USA

Recommind was founded by Professor Thomas Hofmann and Dr Jan Puzicha. The company's main product is Mindserver, which uses probabilistic latent semantic analysis (PLSA) algorithms developed by Hofmann. Unusually, Recommind offers vertical market solutions for federal government, legal, media and life sciences applications.

SAP (ESR)

www.sap.com
(See page 38)

SearchBlox

www.searchblox.com
HQ: Richmond, Virginia, USA

Searchblox was established in 2003 and provides search applications on a J2EE platform using Lucene as the core indexing and search engine.

Siderean (ESR)

http://siderean.com
HQ: El Segundo, California, USA

The company was founded in 2001. Its main product is the Seamark Navigator, which is a faceted search technology. An example of this product in action can be found on the Press Release Navigator section of the Oracle website (http://pressroom.oracle.com/prNavigator.jsp). A range of filters is offered to enable the very large results set of press releases to be progressively refined by adding or removing facets.

Sinequa

www.sinequa.com
HQ: Paris

Sinequa can trace its origins back to Cora, a French software company specializing in linguistic analysis that was founded in 1984. The company changed its name in 2000 and a new management team took over in 2005. The company offers intranet, e-commerce and publisher solutions.

SmartLogic
www.aprsmartlogik.com
HQ: Cambridge, UK

Smartlogic is the trading name of APR Smartlogik Ltd, and offers the Semaphore search software that makes intensive use of taxonomy and ontology approaches. The origin of the company is in the retrieval software developed by Professor Martin Porter for use in the University of Cambridge Department of Geology in the late 1980s, and subsequently commercialized as Muscat. The underlying technology uses a Baysien probability model.

TeraText (ESR)
www.teratext.com
HQ: Melbourne, Australia

TeraText DBS technology was developed at Royal Melbourne Institute of Technology (RMIT) University in Melbourne, Australia, and first commercialized in 1993. It is managed by InQuirion, a spin-off company from the university. In July 2001, SAIC entered into an exclusive agreement with RMIT University to develop and commercialize TeraText technology in North America and Europe, and in September 2005 InQuirion was acquired by Science Applications International Corporation Pty Ltd (SAIC).

Thunderstone (ESR)
www.thunderstone.com
HQ: Cleveland, Ohio, USA

Expansion Programs International Inc. (Thunderstone) is a privately held California corporation that was founded in 1981. TEXIS is a fully integrated SQL RDBMS that intelligently queries and manages databases containing natural language text, standard data types, geographic information, images, video, audio, and other similar data. The other products offered by the company are Webinator, a sophisticated web index and retrieval package, and the Thunderstone search appliance for intranet and enterprise search applications.

Ultraseek (ESR)

www.ultraseek.com

This software product is available through Autonomy following the purchase of Verity Corporation.

Verity (ESR)

www.verity.com

This software product is available through Autonomy following the purchase of Verity Corporation.

Verticrawl

www.verticrawl.com
HQ: Villemomble, France

Verticrawl is a search software product marketed by société Datamean sarl and developed by the French software and services company Velic. It is a Linux-based search application.

Voltix

www.voltix.com
HQ: San Mateo, California, USA

Voltix offers both a desktop search product and also a Java-based enterprise search application. The company was formed from the assets of Exeige, a company founded by Amit Sharma (the CEO of Voltix) in Sydney in 2001. The Chief Technology Officer is Ben van Klinken who was a lead developer of Lucene. The company is also developing the Kshoni collaborative software product, which will enable communities to carry out searches of the content held by members of the community.

Zylab

www.zylab.com
HQ: Vienna, Virginia, USA

Zylab was among the first enterprise search companies and was founded in 1983, introducing ZyINDEX, the first full-text retrieval software for the personal computer, in the same year. The focus of the company's products is on information retrieval applications for document and records management applications, with an emphasis on compliance and anti-fraud requirements.

Further reading

In this section:

The resources cover a range of topics related to search, and complement the references given at the end of each chapter.

Websites

Search tools for websites and intranets

www.searchtools.com
This site is maintained by Avi Rappoport and offers comprehensive lists of search engines, useful articles, and links to just about everything of importance on the practice and technology of searching. The best place to start, without a doubt.

New Idea Engineering

www.ideaeng.com/pub/entsrch/index.html
New Idea Engineering was founded in 1996 to provide technical consulting, training and programming to companies implementing search technologies from Verity, Ultraseek, Fulcrum Technologies and Autonomy. The company

is based in Cupertino, near San Francisco. The site offers a good enterprise search newsletter.

eWeek

www.eweek.com/category2/0,1874,1740156,00.asp
eWeek has regular features on developments in web and enterprise search.

Step Two Designs

www.steptwo.com.au/papers/index.php?subject=searchtools
James Robertson writes very practical papers on search topics, including:

- what to include in intranet search results
- intranet search reports
- deploying an effective search engine.

Enterprise Search Center

www.enterprisesearchcenter.com/
This was set up by Information Today Inc. as a resource centre for the enterprise search community. Information Today has announced the publication in 2007 of the first annual *Enterprise Search Sourcebook*.

On Search – the Series

www.tbray.org/ongoing/When/200x/2003/07/30/OnSearchTOC
A set of 15 essays on various aspects of information retrieval by Tim Bray, who developed search software for OpenText Corp and was a leader in the development of XML.

Blogs

Barney Pell's Web Log

www.barneypell.com/
Barney Pell is the CEO of PowerSet, a start-up search engine company, and writes on natural language search issues.

John Batelle's Searchblog

http://battellemedia.com
The emphasis is on website search, but given the entry of the web search vendors into desktop search, this is a good source of news and opinion.

Searchmax

http://searchmax.blogspot.com/
This is the blog of Dave Goebel, the Chief Executive of the Goebel Group, and covers both web and enterprise search developments.

Unstruct.Org

www.unstruct.org/
This blog covers a range of search topics and is published by the Swedish consultancy Infosphere.

Conferences

There are three search-specific conferences that take place each year, and two more general conferences that have a strong focus on search applications.

Search Engine Meeting

www.infonortics.com/searchengines/index.html
This is organized by Infonortics and usually takes place in Boston in April each year.

The papers cover new technical developments in both web and enterprise searching. Most of the papers given at the event from 2001 onwards can be downloaded from the website.

Enterprise Search Summit

www.infotoday.com
The Summit is organized by Information Today Inc. and takes place in May each year. The first Summit took place in New York in 2004.

Enterprise Information Management

www.wbresearch.com/eimusa/index.asp
This conference took place in San Franscisco in January 2007.

Online Information Conference

www.online-information.co.uk
There is an Enterprise Search track at the Online Information Conference held in London in early December each year.

KM World/Intranets

www.kmworld.com/kmw05/
The KM World and Intranets conference takes place in San Jose in November each year, and there are always papers on intranet and enterprise search implementation.

Books

Arnold, S. (2005) *The Google Legacy*, Tetbury, Infonortics Ltd, www.infonortics.com/publications/google/google-legacy.html.
Rosenfeld, L. and Morville, P. (2006) *Information Architecture for the World Wide Web*, 3rd edn, Sebastopol CA, O'Reilly Publishing, www.oreilly.com.

Research Reports

CMS Watch (www.cmswatch.com) publishes a range of reports which offer detailed evaluations of software products. The reports relevant to the topic of search are the following. They are revised on a regular basis.

- the Enterprise Portals Report
- the Enterprise Search Report
- the CMS Report
- the Text Mining Report (first edition to be published in 2007)
- the Web Analytics Report (first edition to be published in 2007).

In 2003 the Swedish consulting company Infosphere AB (www.infosphere.se) published a report entitled *Unstructured Information Management*. Although the profiles of the vendors in the report are no longer current the methodology used in the report to assess the vendors is still useful, as are the sections on search technology.

The following consultancy organizations also publish reports on the search software industry but these reports are only available to clients of the company and cannot be purchased on an individual basis.

- Forrester Research (www.forrester.com)
- Gartner Group (www.gartner.com)
- International Data Corporation (www.idc.com)
- Butler Group (www.butlergroup.com).

Glossary

Access control list (ACL) Defines which employees have access to specific servers and/or documents.

Algorithm A procedure consisting of a finite set of instructions for accomplishing a task which, on the basis of the initial input, will terminate in a defined end-state.

Appliance A search product that consists of integrated software and hardware in a box that can be inserted directly into a server rack.

Application programming interface (API) Provides a means of linking two different software programs together.

Boolean search Uses the operators AND, OR and NOT to create a query term from two or more individual words.

Concurrent users Two or more people logged into and using the same application.

Content management system (CMS) Software program used to manage the content of websites and intranets.

Crawler A software element that accesses web and other servers to identify content that should be indexed.

Federated search A search system that works across multiple applications and/or multiple search applications to produce an integrated search result.

Findability The quality of being locatable or navigable (Peter Morville).

Legacy database Often used to denote databases (and applications) that are not run under the current information systems architecture.

Lemmatization The use of language-specific rules and dictionaries to recognize different grammatical versions of a word.

Metadata Information added to a document about the subject of the document, the author, and other elements that is not already explicitly defined in the text of the document.

Natural language processing (NLP) Use of linguistic analysis to derive meaning from a document that is not explicitly expressed by the words in the document.

Precision The number of relevant hits/the number of documents in the list.

Query One or more words used to initiate a search.

Ranking Ordering a list according to a set of rules, such as by date.

Recall The number of relevant hits/number of relevant documents in the collection.

Relevance A subjective assessment of the value of a document to a user.

Repository Used as a synonym for one of more servers containing content that can be searched.

Scalability The ability of a computer system to cope with additional applications or transactions.

Search engine Often used to describe search software products.

Taxonomy A hierarchical arrangement of terms in which each term is placed in a unique position that is contextually correct with respect to other terms in the hierarchy.

Vector space model Each term and each document in which the terms are found is calculated as a vector using a formula in which the components are the frequency in which the term occurred in the document, the number of documents containing the term, and the total number of documents in the set.

Subject index

Company index